KALILA AND DIMNA

KALILA AND DIMNA

SELECTED FABLES OF BIDPAI

RETOLD BY RAMSAY WOOD
ILLUSTRATED BY MARGARET KILRENNY

ALFRED·A·KNOPF NEW YORK 1980

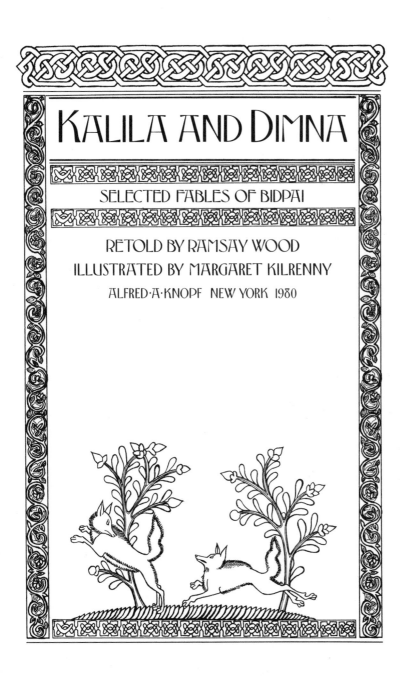

This is a Borzoi Book published by Alfred A. Knopf, Inc.
Copyright © 1980 by Ramsay Wood
All rights reserved under International and Pan-American
Copyright Conventions. Published in the United States
by Alfred A. Knopf, Inc., New York, and simultaneously
in Canada by Random House of Canada Limited, Toronto.
Distributed by Random House, Inc., New York.
Library of Congress Cataloging in Publication Data
Wood, Ramsay. (Date)   Kalila and Dimna: selected fables of Bidpai.
1. Fables. I. Bídpá'í. Persian version. Anvár-i Suhaylí.
English. Selections. II. Title.
PN989.I5B4 1980   398.2′452   79-17425
ISBN 0-394-50693-6
Manufactured in the United States of America   First Edition

This book

is dedicated to its many midwives,

including al·Kashifi, who in the preface

to his fifteenth·century Persian version

of this story described himself as

"this contemptible atom

of but small intellectual store."

 CONTENTS

CONTENTS

Introduction

The claim has been made for this book that it has
travelled more widely than the Bible, for it has been
translated through the centuries everywhere from
Ethiopia to China. Yet it is safe to say that most people
in the West these days will not have heard of it, while
they will certainly at the very least have heard of the
Upanishads and the *Vedas*. Until comparatively recently, it was the other way around. Anyone with any
claim to a literary education knew that the *Fables of
Bidpai*, or the *Tales of Kalila and Dimna* — these being
the most commonly used titles with us — was a great
Eastern classic. There were at least twenty English
translations in the hundred years before 1888. Pondering on these facts leads to reflection on the fate of
books, as chancy and unpredictable as that of people
or nations.

The book's history is as fascinating as its contents,
and would make a pretty volume on its own.

The first English translation was done in the six-
teenth century by Sir Thomas North — he who translated Plutarch into a work which was the source of

Shakespeare's knowledge of the Roman world. North's Plutarch was popular reading; so was his version of *Bidpai*. In the introduction to the re-issue of this translation in the nineteenth century, Joseph Jacobs of Cambridge (Jews have been prominent in the history of the movement and adaptation of the book) concludes: "If I go on further, I foresee a sort of mental dialogue which will pass between my reader and myself: 'What,' the reader will exclaim, 'the first literary link between India and England, between Buddhism and Christendom, written in racy English with vivacious dialogue and something resembling a plot. Why, you will be trying to make us believe that you have restored to us an English Classic!' 'Exactly so,' I should be constrained to reply, and lest I be tempted into this temerity, I will even make a stop here."

And he did stop, but by then he had written a very great number of pages. I have been handed over by Ramsay Wood a vast heap of many versions of the *Fables of Bidpai*—some of them rare and precious—to aid me in this task of doing an introduction, and the first thing to be noticed is that the introductions tend to be very long: it is clear that the authors of them have become beguiled and besotted with the book's history. As I have. For one thing, it has lasted at least two thousand years. But it is hard to say where the beginning was—suitably for a book whose nature it is to accommodate tales within tales and to blur the margins between historical fact and fiction.

One progenitor was the Buddhist cycle of Birth Tales (or Jātaka Stories) where the Buddha appears as a monkey, deer, lion, and so on. Several of the Bidpai tales came from this cycle. Incidents that occur in *Bidpai* can be seen in sculptures around Buddhist shrines dated before 200 B.C. The Buddha himself took some of the Birth Tales from earlier folktales about animals. But there is no race or nation from the Egyptians on—or back, for we may surely no longer assume that current information regarding ancient history is all there is to be known, or all that we will come to know—that has not used beast-fables as part of its heritage of instructional material. And so the genre is as ancient as mankind itself. Sir Richard Burton, who like all the other orientalists of the nineteenth century was involved with *Bidpai,* suggested that man's use of the beast-fable commemorates our instinctive knowledge of how we emerged from the animal kingdom, on two legs but still with claws and fangs.

Another source or contributor was that extraordinary book, the *Arthaśāstra* of Kautilya, which is suspected of dating from about 300 B.C. It is not easy to lay one's hands on a copy, and this is a pity: at a time when we are all, down to the least citizen, absorbed, not to say obsessed, with sociology and the arts of proper government, this book should take its place, not as the earliest manual on the subject, but as the earliest we know of. It describes in exact and even pernickety detail how properly to run a kingdom, from the kind of goods that should be available in the marketplace to the choice of kingly advisers; how one should go about creating a new village, and where; the right way to employ artisans to manufacture gold and silver coins; disputes between neighbours about property and boundaries; how to keep accounts; the legal system; the use of spies. It is all here. And to our minds, what a mixture of humanity and brutality! It was forbidden, for instance, to have sex with a woman against her will, even if she was a prostitute, but there are also lengthy instructions about the use of torture as a punishment. Kautilya was a very cool one indeed; surely this book must have influenced Machiavelli when he wrote *The Prince.* If not, then the books come from the same region of human experience. Candid, unrhetorical, infinitely worldly-wise, the tone is more like that which one imagines must exist, let's say, between a Begin and a Sadat when sitting together facing the realities of a situation unobserved by slogan-chanting supporters, or between a Churchill and a Roosevelt meeting in the middle of a war. There is nothing in the *Arthaśāstra* that minimizes the harshness of necessary choices. It was by no means the first of such handy guides to statesmanship, for Kautilya says it is a compendium of "almost all the *Arthaśāstras* which in view of acquisition and maintenance of the earth have been composed by ancient teachers." In other words, this to us so ancient book was to him the last in a long line of instructive tracts, stretching back into antiquity. Throughout he quotes the view of this one or that, sometimes up to ten or more, and then adds at the end, "My teacher says . . ." but usually disagrees with them all, including his teacher, with "No, says Kautilya . . ." or "Not so, says Kautilya . . ." setting everything and everyone right, so that the book has about it the air of a young man refusing to be impressed by tradition—rather like students in the sixties bringing their own books to class and insisting on choosing their own curriculum.

The cycle called *The Fables of Bidpai* came into existence in this manner . . . but let us choose a version that, typically, tries to set fiction on a base of fact. Alexander the Great, having conquered India, set a disliked and unjust governor over the vanquished ones, who were at last able to overturn this tyrant, and chose a ruler of their own. This was King Dabschelim, but he turned out to be no better than his predecessor. A wise and incorruptible sage named Bidpai, knowing that he risked his life, went to the no-good King to tell him that the heavens were displeased with him because of his depredations, his cruelties, his refusal to be properly responsible for the welfare of the people put in his care. And sure enough, Bidpai found himself cast into the deepest and foulest dungeon; but the King, attracting to himself heavenly influences because of his inner disquiet over this behaviour of his, was caused to think again and . . . Thereafter the tale unfolds in the characteristic way of the genre, stories within stories, one leading to another. We in the West do not have this kind of literature, except where it has come to us through influences from the East: Boccaccio and Chaucer, for instance. What this method of story-telling, or this design, is supposed to illustrate is the way that in life one thing leads to another, often unexpectedly, and that one may not make neat and tidy containers for ideas and events—or hopes and possibilities—and that it is not easy to decide where anything begins or ends. As the history of the book itself proves. When the "frame" story stops, temporarily, and a cluster of related tales are told, what is happening is that many facets of a situation are being illuminated, before the movement of the main story goes on. There may be even more than one "frame" story, so that we are led gently into realm after realm, doors opening as if one were to push a mirror and find it a door.

Another version of the book's origin is that there was once a good and honest King who had three stupid and lazy sons. Many educational experts came forward with suggestions as to their proper instruction, but the King was in despair, knowing that to give them the foundation of information they needed would take years, by which time the kingdom would be ruined. And then came a sage who said he would impart to the three princes the essence of statesmanship and sensible conduct in the form of instructive fables, and the process would be accomplished in a very short time, if the princes could be persuaded to pay attention. Thus the book has been known as *A Mirror for Princes*, and we are told that it was given to princes as part of their training to be monarchs.

The original Sanskrit version vanished, though later the material was translated back into Sanskrit from other languages, and India has produced as many versions "as there are stars in the sky." The ancient Persian King of Kings, Nushirvan, heard of the book, and sent embassies, and it was translated into the ancient

Persian tongue of Pahlevi, which event was thought of such importance that Firdausi celebrated it in the *Shahnama*. The incidents of the tales were infinitely illustrated in this book and in very many others, and anyone at all interested in Persian art will certainly have come across them in miniatures and otherwise. Not only Persian art—I have here a postcard from the British Museum of a turtle being carried through the air on a stick by two geese: the friends who could not bear to be parted. It is from a Turkish manuscript. The British Museum has this and many other ancient manuscripts so precious one may view them only through glass, like jewels, which they resemble.

When the Arabs conquered the old world, after the death of Mohammed, poets and scholars arrived in India, enquiring for the famous book they had heard so much about. The way they tracked it down, like the account of how the old Persian envoys found their copy, makes an attractive story full of suspense, mystery, and drama, so that one has to suspect that the storytellers of the time took their opportunity to honour even further this honoured book by copious invention; while some of them made "quest tales" from the material, in which the book becomes a hidden treasure. The most famous translation into Arabic was by a Zoroastrian who converted to Islam. Another was probably by an honoured Jewish scholar. In those comparatively flexible days, scholars were able more easily than now to appreciate each other and work together across boundaries. There were religions then, not nations—a fact it is hard to remember in its dimensions when considering how things were in those days. For instance, to read the biography of Mohammed by ibn-Ishaq, the Moslem equivalent of the New Testament, where nations and national feelings are absent, and men and women are known as Moslems, Jews, Christians, Zoroastrians, and there were no Arabs and Jews in our sense, since that is a division of modern times, to read this book is hard for a modern Westerner because of how we see everything in terms of nations and nationalism. So strange is it that the mind keeps seizing up and you have to stop, and start again.

The query has been raised: What was the "secret ingredient" of this Bidpai book, "this ocean of tales," that enabled it to be absorbed without resistance, and to be loved by Buddhists, Zoroastrians, Christians, Moslems, Jews? One answer was that in all these traditions it is established that tales and parables are for instruction and illustration as well as for entertainment. Medieval Europe rushed to translate the book because its fame was known, and they wanted its aid in learning how to live better. But nowadays we use this phrase in a different sense.

One of the best-known and most influential of the old versions was *Anwar-i-Suhaili,* or *The Lights of Canopus.* There had been earlier Persian versions, but these were considered inadequate and even elitist. An emir, or general, called Suhaili (of Canopus) invited one al-Kashifi to make a new version. I was interested that Canopus was being used as a name in a culture and at a time when names were often chosen to describe qualities, or as an indication of qualities a person hoped to

acquire. People were expected to regard names as
signposts, as it were. Round about that time there
came into existence a cluster of Persian classics, all of
Sufic origin and inspiration. *The Lights of Suhaili* is
one of these. It is the same in "feel" and format as, for
instance, Saadi's *Rose Garden*, using the Bidpai tales
as a frame, or lattice, around which are woven associated tales, anecdotes, reminiscences, current scientific
information, and verse of different kinds. It is worth-
while insisting that this great classic, now regarded
with a truly horrible reverence and solemnity, was a
popular book, meant for entertainment, as well as instruction. But who was this general or governor whose
name became the name of the book, so that he was, in
the way of those times and regions, place, person, tradition—all at once—and was able to bring about the
creation of a new Sufi classic, using the ancient Bidpai
material to do it? And who was al-Kashifi, whose name
means "that which is manifested," or "shown," or
"demonstrated"?

Canopus the star is much embedded in the mythol-
ogy of ancient times and when you trace it to this
country or that it melds and merges into other names,
places, personages. To illustrate the remarkable law
known to all researchers, but not yet acknowledged by
science—that when one is becoming interested in a
subject, books formerly unknown and unsuspected fly
to your hand from everywhere—while I was speculat-
ing about Canopus, and what it could mean in this
context, if it meant anything, there came my way *Astronomical Curiosities*, published in 1909, and one of

its main sources of information was one al-Sufi, an Arabian astronomer of the tenth century. Much is said by al-Sufi about Canopus of the constellation Argo. Argo was associated with Noah's Ark. It represents, too, the first ship ever built, which was in Thessaly, by order of Minerva and Neptune, to go on the expedition for the conquest of the Golden Fleece. The date of this expedition commanded by Jason is usually fixed at 1300 or 1400 B.C. Canopus was the ancient name of Aboukir in Egypt, and is said to have derived its name from the pilot of Menelaus, whose name was Kanobus, and who died there "from the bite of a snake." The star is supposed to have been named after him, in some traditions, and it was worshipped by the ancient Egyptians . . . but Canopus is also the god Osiris, and is in the most remarkable and ever-changing relationship with Isis, who was the star Sirius . . . and thus is one enticed into all kinds of byways, from which it is hard to extricate oneself, and harder still to resist quoting, and thus joining the immoderate preface-makers whom I can no longer in honesty condemn.

The *Iliad* and *Odyssey* are linked with Bidpai in another way too: a Greek called Seth Simeon translated it in the eleventh century, adding to it all kinds of bits and pieces from these two epics—another illustration, if one is needed by now, of the way such material adapts to new backgrounds and new times. In Hebrew, Turkish, Latin, Russian, Malay, Polish—in almost any language you can think of—its naturalization followed the laws of infinite adaptability. It is not possible to trace its influences: as is always the way when a book's seminal power has been great, it was absorbed and transformed by local cultures. Certainly the Bidpai tales can be found in the folklore of most European countries, almost as much as they can in the East. Some were adapted by La Fontaine. Beaumont and Fletcher are supposed to have used *The Dervish and the Thief* as a germ for *Women Pleased*. Aesop's fables as we know them are indebted to Bidpai.

There has not been an English version for a long time. The existing ones have become stiff and boring. Many consider Sir Thomas North's still to be the best, but what for the Elizabethans was a lively new book is for us a museum piece.

This fresh creation by Ramsay Wood follows the more than two-thousand-year-old precedent of adapting, collating, and arranging the old material in any way that suits present purposes. It is contemporary, racy, vigorous, full of zest. It is also very funny. I defy anyone to sit down with it and not finish it at a sitting; his own enjoyment in doing the book has made it so enjoyable.

And there is another good thing. The original, or perhaps I should say some arrangements of the original, had thirteen sections: The Separation of Friends, The Winning of Friends, War and Peace, The Loss of One's Gains, The Rewards of Impatience, and so forth. This volume has only the material to do with friends, artfully arranged to make a whole. And so we may look forward—I hope—to the rest.

Doris Lessing

KALILA AND DIMNA

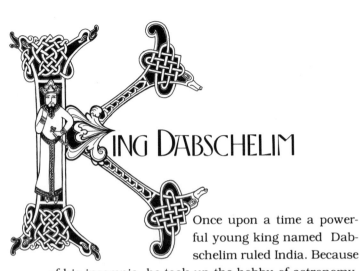

KING DABSCHELIM

Once upon a time a power-
ful young king named Dab-
schelim ruled India. Because
of his insomnia, he took up the hobby of astronomy.
Adjacent to the Royal Bedchamber he built an observatory, partially open to the sky and equipped with the
best mechanisms that the wise could devise. It con-
tained a beautifully wrought brass astrolabe, intri-
cately fashioned and embellished with pleasing designs of inlaid silver, studded here and there on the
rotating alidade by marking points of tiny rubies or
diamonds; handsome, heavy rulers and protractors
of the thickest ivory; golden callipers; the best star
maps, drawn on the finest vellum—rolled and stored in
delicately hand-carved ebony canisters; an amazing
armillary sphere; a clepsydra; and many other intri-
guing instruments. King Dabschelim passed his sleep-
less nights studying the heavenly bodies. He was entranced by the silent music of the spheres and spent
hours observing positions of star and planet, taking
readings of individual celestial altitude and azimuth,

3

computing problems of spherical astronomy, and carefully inking these measurements upon his personal maps. Or, sometimes, if the mood struck him, he would simply sit in his favourite chair and gaze at the moon.

Whatever he was doing, at some point, usually in the early hours of the morning, he would yawn and squint his eyes and begin to nod his head, whereupon his retainers would rush forward, catch him firmly under the arms, and lead him through the doorway into the Royal Bedchamber. He would be quickly undressed and tucked in with Wife of the Night, who by this time was normally sound asleep.

One night Dabschelim was lucky enough to witness a spectacular shooting star. It began brightly near the zenith of the sky, streaked down across the darkness with a bright tail of sparks, and suddenly fizzled out well above the horizon. Even one of the king's retainers, a pleasant though doltish fellow, felt compelled to gasp at such a breathtaking sight.

In those days astronomy and astrology were linked like twins. It was simply unheard of for anyone to be interested in stars and planetary movements and not simultaneously be keen on trying to predict the future. But King Dabschelim wasn't very interested in astrology. Oh, he listened to what the greybearded soothsayers said about Houses of the Zodiac, ascendant signs, and how the gods spoke to men about future events through variations in planetary position and aspect. And Dabschelim was cautious enough to play along with his various court astrologers and their consensus of prediction; he always let them draw up their little charts to select auspicious dates before launching any new enterprise, and he listened to their advice about his personal life as well. But he didn't really believe it. No, he thought astrology was . . . well, there was nothing exactly wrong with it, but somehow it seemed too loose, too imprecise; there were always so many possible interpretations from the evidence of what he himself could observe in the night skies.

In any case, Dabschelim didn't particularly care about the future. After all, he was king and could do pretty much what he wanted. He hardly even considered the future. He liked living now and not worrying about what might or might not happen later. Whenever his astrologers predicted something that did not accord with his whim, he simply ignored them and went ahead with his own plans. He was the king, you see, and could have their heads chopped off if he felt like it. So the greybeards tended not to argue with him very much if he ignored their suggestions.

Yet on the night when he saw this shooting star, even King Dabschelim felt a twinge of apprehension. It was so dramatic that even he thought it must be a sign. But a sign of what? He abandoned the golden callipers in his hand and sat down in his favourite chair to stare at the moon. At first, he was very excited and ran his attention over all the peculiar irregularities of the moon's surface. Everything seemed so mysterious, so complicated and strange. And then, slowly, in a more peaceful mood, he simply drifted into wondering, in a vague way, what this vast universe signified. The moon gazed down on him.

"Why," he mused to himself, "did I, Dabschelim, see that shooting star tonight? What, if anything, does it mean?" He yawned, nodded his head, and began to doze off.

Immediately his retainers were at his elbows and lifting him up. Dabschelim's feet shuffled across the marble floor of the observatory as he was led into the Royal Bedchamber. He felt very, very heavy.

"Amazing, most amazing," he muttered to himself several times.

Gently they put him into his bed next to one of his most delectable wives, a dark, ravishing, long-haired beauty whose eyes, highlighted by the most deft application of kohl, shone brightly in the obscurity of the room. Yes, she was fully awake to receive her king, and tenderly folded her arms around his body. Dabschelim fell into the deepest sleep and dreamed.

It was a peculiarly strong dream. Dabschelim found himself sitting at a table in his observatory, pondering some stellar configuration. And then a stranger interrupted him. The man wore an immaculate green robe and approached quickly without any of the usual deferential bowing and scraping. His face and his garment seemed to shimmer with their own inner glow and he moved with supreme confidence. Instinctively Dabschelim drew back in his seat, fearing for one horrible moment that he was about to meet the lunge of an assassin. But the figure stopped short and spoke:

"Fear not, O King! My purpose is to congratulate, not harm you. The diligence with which you ponder our inscrutable heavens constitutes the single laudable feature of your reign to date and, as such, deserves encouragement. Therefore I have come to reward you from the source of reward, if you can but focus your attention upon the clues I shall give.''

Dabschelim sat frozen with astonishment, unable to speak, barely breathing. Except for his father, who had preceded him as king, hardly anyone had ever dared to address him in so forthright a manner. He noticed that his grip on the chair arms had tightened. The man in green stepped back a pace, crossed his arms over his chest, and continued in a full and resonant voice:

"Remember to remember the meteor you witnessed tonight," he said firmly. "By their vastness the heavens give even a king an inkling of his stupidity. You were quite right to pause and wonder, Dabschelim, for there are some things you will never know. That shooting star is yourself, O King—a mere atom of a moment's span. And will you too, O Bright and Powerful One, vanish in the darkness without the slightest trace?''

The apparition paused and slowly fingered its beard while regarding Dabschelim with the barest hint of a smile. Then it leaned right across the table on its elbows and propped its face in its hands. Dabschelim suddenly felt the coolness of the green man's breath upon his cheeks and gasped, but then he relaxed and exhaled normally. Despite their nearness, the eyes that bore deeply into his own were mysteriously soothing.

"I come to tell you of a treasure rich beyond your dreams," said the face before him softly. "Ride at dawn tomorrow into the mountains of the northeast towards

Zindawar and seek this treasure before it is too late. If you are worthy, you will find it and learn how to be truly rich, and not the ignorant pauper-king that you in truth are—a king blinded by the pleasures of power and soon to disappear without benefit to anyone. Go, now—you to your world and I to mine." The green man drew back and simply walked out of the room.

Dabschelim later would recall a final sensation of sitting slumped in his chair feeling neither happy nor sad, but simultaneously hopeful and utterly powerless.

He awoke refreshed the next morning before sunrise and immediately rose to prepare for the journey suggested in his dream. It remained so vivid an experience that everywhere he looked he saw the green man's glowing face staring back at him, as if from a mirror.

"Your Majesty has only had a few hours of sleep and surely must need more rest," said his wife from the depths of the royal bed.

"I'm all right," answered the king with a smile. "Why don't you go back to sleep, my beauty?" Which she did.

Dabschelim issued various orders throughout the palace and by dawn he had successfully roused a few courtiers, a couple of sleepy ministers, and a small contingent of cavalry for an unexpected trip. They rode off towards the northeast, rode all day and most of the day after—up the flood-scoured valley of the mighty Indus. The second night they spent at Chaudwan, and on the third morning followed a flashing tributary up into the mountains until they saw Zindawar perched like a nest among the barren foothills.

Many black-mouthed caves yawned from the mountain face that swept off into the clouds from behind the town. As they rode on, Dabschelim noticed a solitary man sitting in the entrance of a cave nearby. Deciding that he might as well begin his search here as anywhere else, he turned his horse off the track and approached. Almost immediately, as if he knew the king's desire, the hermit leapt up and came forward with long, purposeful strides.

A sudden surge of hope overwhelmed Dabschelim when he beheld the jaunty manner in which this venerable one moved to pay his respects. The king dismounted, handed his reins to a retainer, and went to meet the hermit.

"Sire, Sire," cried the hermit, as he bounded over the last few rocks that separated them, "it gives my heart great joy to behold your bejewelled turban draw nigh; yesyes—great joy! The Mightiest King of the East approaches the miserable hovel of his meanest subject, hee hee—me, me!" He paused to catch his breath, beaming an indescribably radiant smile towards Dabschelim, a smile so infectious it was impossible not to return it. This gesture of pleasure from Dabschelim fired the old man's gaiety even more, and, with the unkempt beard that hung down to his middle swinging crazily from side to side, he commenced prancing and jumping about, first on one foot and then the other, whirling around in little circles of happiness.

"Yesyes," he sang out as he danced, "it is in accordance with custom. Great kings come to visit the poor, it's true. They do, they do! Great kings become greater, yesyes. It augments their grandeur. All praise! All praise to the Unseen Powers which govern men's affairs! I knew this was my lucky day; I knew it!''

A portly minister appeared by the royal elbow and whispered something into the king's ear to the effect that perhaps Your Highness ought to withdraw to a safer distance in view of the potential danger to Your Personage from the unpredictability of this mad fellow, etcetera, etcetera. Dabschelim did not even deign to turn around, but merely shooed this voice of caution away with a few gentle flicks from the littlest finger of his right hand. The minister retired several paces, but remained close by in case of an emergency.

"Come, come, O King—come and visit me," the hermit called out in his singsong voice, hopping about and waving Dabschelim forward. "You live in a palace, and I live in a cave, haha! Please, please, O King—accept my hospitality. Come, come!''

"All right," said Dabschelim in a firm voice for everyone to hear, "I'm coming.''

He turned and frowned at his band of followers, indicating very clearly that he wished them to remain behind and not interfere. The portly minister swept his eyes and the palms of his hands heavenwards, shrugged himself into a brief pose of helplessness before the Almighty, and turned with many slow shakes of his head to rejoin his colleagues.

Thus it was that King Dabschelim, dressed in the finest silks, with several large dazzling rings bedecking each hand, his lower legs wound spirally with white puttees of the softest leather, and his body exuding the most pleasing whiffs of rosewater scent, walked up the hill following a skinny old beggar whose nakedness was barely concealed by an old loincloth.

"Sire," said the hermit once they were in the cave, "it is not for the likes of me to offer Your Majesty any refreshment. No, no—that would not do! Only cracked mugs exist in this home, and they, to be sure, are unworthy to receive the lips of a great king. But I do have a present for you, My Liege—yesyes, I do, I do. If it pleases you to accept it, if it pleases you."

"Don't worry, old man," Dabschelim responded. "I am not the least bit thirsty. I am enjoying your company and would be delighted to accept your gift. What is it?"

"Aha, Your Majesty; it's a treasure, you see—a hidden treasure. And, moreover, Sire, it is a special treasure earmarked for King Dabschelim alone from long, long ago—yesyes. My father's father told him, 'Keep the treasure until King Dabschelim accepts it,' and my father told me, you see? It's been a sacred trust in our family for many generations, yesyes—going back to even before the father of my great-great-grandfather. 'Keep the bequest for King Dabschelim.' That is what we have always been told, from father to son. And since you are, of course, King Dabschelim, then I must offer it to you, yesyes—I must, I must! It is my duty!"

"Good heavens, man!" expostulated the king. "Where is it?"

"Ah, well—I'm not too sure of that, Sire," answered the hermit. He waved an arm in a vague semicircle to indicate the general area above the cave. "It's around

here somewhere, though; yesyes, I'm sure of that. My
father told me so. But I can't tell you exactly where,
you see, because I don't know—I don't, I don't. Command your servants to seek it, Sire. Yesyes, give the
order to search for the treasure. It will be found, it will
be found."

Dabschelim strode to the entrance of the cave and
hailed his men below. In no time they had galloped up
on their horses. He divided the group into small search
parties and commanded them to seek for a treasure
nearby. Soon the men were digging and poking about
in every conceivable spot around the cave. The king
stepped back inside.

"Your gift is truly remarkable," he said to the hermit. "And I shall tell you why."

Dabschelim sat down on a rock and told the old man
all about the night of the shooting star and his dream.
It was the first time he had spoken of his dream to
anyone, but he felt sure he could confide in this hermit.

"Aha, yesyes. It all makes sense, Sire—it does, it
does!" the old man exclaimed when the king had finished speaking. "My gift is in conformity with the supreme will of the Unseen Powers—all praise, all
praise!"

At that moment there was a great shout from the
men outside, and the portly minister rushed in.

"Your Majesty," he said breathlessly, "come
quickly, please. We have found something amazing!"

For once, the portly minister was not exaggerating.
The men had heaved aside a huge boulder from the
hillside to reveal a small cave. It opened with a low,

narrow mouth, just large enough to crawl through, but inside the roof sheared up high enough for a man to stand. And when Dabschelim crouched to peer into its interior, he could see dozens of old coffers neatly stacked against the back wall. They were hauled out into the sunlight and opened one by one with growing excitement. A dream come true. Gold, silver, jewels— enough to dazzle the mind.

Dabschelim sat in a daze, running his fingers through a priceless heap of rubies, diamonds, emeralds, opals, and myriad other gems, again and again letting them dribble back towards their treàsure chest in a glittering stream of flashing lights. The hermit hopped and skipped about with even more vigour, bouncing all over the place and kicking his bare heels in the air with an agility truly remarkable for one of such advanced years.

"All praise! All praise! Yesyes, all praise!" he chanted.

But there was one strongbox which no one could open. It was extremely heavy, strengthened by iron bands, and firmly padlocked in six different places. Dabschelim grew so curious about this particular strongbox that he dispatched horsemen to Zindawar with instructions to fetch back a smith to open it immediately. In the meantime, he organized an inventory of the mammoth treasure. All the rubies were put into one coffer, all the diamonds in another, and so forth, with the gold and silver heaped in huge mounds upon the ground.

Eventually the smith arrived and commenced work

on the stubborn strongbox. After some difficulty he
succeeded in sawing through the padlocks. When
Dabschelim lifted the lid, he was intrigued to discover
yet another strongbox, more luxurious, solid silver
with complex gold inlay designs covering every surface. Altogether such a wonder of craftsmanship that it
seemed a pity to tamper with it. But there was no other
way to fathom the mystery, and so once again the
smith set to work. At length this box too was opened,
revealing yet a third, this time a casket of gold,
adorned with the largest and most precious diamonds
and rubies that the king had ever seen. There was a
golden key in the lock. Dabschelim turned it and raised
the lid. Inside was a roll of white satin tied with a
purple ribbon and sealed with wax.

Dabschelim broke the seal and pulled off the ribbon.
The strip of satin was quite long, its inner surface covered with masterful calligraphy and sealed at the bottom by the same mark which had attached the ribbon.
The writing, however, was an ancient language which
nobody could read.

"This is getting ridiculous," Dabschelim remarked
with a laugh. He sat down on a nearby chest and puz-
zled over the strange writing, unable to make head or
tail of it. His ministers, courtiers, and horsemen
crowded around him offering their advice and interpretations. Some thought the document was a magic
talisman designed to protect the treasure; others spec-
ulated that it was the last will and testament of the
owner; others said it might be a curse and potentially
dangerous; and there were other opinions as well.

Soon all the king's men were arguing and debating among themselves, each trying to convince the others of his point of view.

"Silence!" roared Dabschelim. "All this blether is getting us nowhere. We need a translator who understands this language. Mount up and search Zindawar and its outskirts for a scholar, a linguist who reads the ancient languages. I don't want any excuses. Find me a linguist quickly! Then we will know what this writing means and we can stop clucking away like a bunch of old hens. I'll wait here with the old man. Now begone with you."

"But, Sire," began the portly minister, after stepping forward and bowing a very low bow, "do you think it is wise for Your Majesty to remain here alone with all this treasure? Would it not be more prudent perhaps for at least a few of us to stay behind as guards to protect Your Highness?"

"You heard me," the king answered in such a low, unrelenting tone that his startled minister stumbled backward a full pace. "Stop dawdling!" he snapped. "I shall be all right on my own. Mount up and be off with you, and don't come back without that linguist!"

They all rode off quickly towards Zindawar, raising a haze of dust that spread out across the landscape behind them, while Dabschelim rolled up the satin strip and carefully tucked it away on his person.

The king's men were lucky. After a diligent search they tracked down a man from Shinghar who was visiting relatives and who, so rumour had it, was a formidable scholar. They brought him back, a thin little man with a pinched face riding pillion behind the Captain of Horse.

The scholar's name was Farsi, and when he smiled, which was frequently, only his bottom teeth showed, as if in a grimace. But whatever his appearance, he knew his stuff; there was soon no doubt of that. He sat on a treasure chest and pored over the cryptic scroll while Dabschelim paced back and forth impatiently.

"Hmm, yes . . . very interesting, Your Majesty, very interesting indeed," Farsi said without looking up. "This language is ancient Syriac, dating from the Houschenk period—as authenticated by the seal, no doubt. Let me see, now: 'Hre-ta-char-me-ku. . . .' No, no, that's not right. Ummm . . . 'Kwa'! Yes, it's definitely a 'Kwa.' Uhh . . . 'Kwa-shon-pee-na-tuni.' Hmm . . . ah, yes, of course. Now then: 'Ki-ti-me-coso-na-ra-ta-par-sni-rue-bar . . .' "

He went on muttering and mumbling to himself this way for many minutes. Every now and again he would tug his beard or bite a lip or screw up his eyes and tap his chin with two fingers or throw his head back as if scanning the skies for some obscure clue. The men milled about him respectfully, glancing at the scroll over his shoulder and silently urging him forward over the thorny passages. At length the scholar's lower lip dropped into his peculiar smile, and he stood up to face the king.

"Your Highness, this document is truly a treasure on its own. It is a letter from the great King Houschenk, long dead, to yourself—a most amazing fact in itself, but never mind that. What King Houschenk offers you here is specific guidance for achieving greatness as a king. He lists a series of precepts which he suggests a king would be wise to follow. If you wish, Your Majesty, I shall endeavour to read the letter aloud. I think I've got the gist of it now, but I must warn you that it is fairly long."

Dabschelim nodded his assent. Farsi, after clearing his throat, read slowly and clearly as follows:

"*Dear King of the Future,*

I, King Houschenk, have buried this treasure for the future use of the great King Dabschelim. It has been revealed to me in a vision that only he will be fit to manage it according to the intention of its design.

Amid all this preposterous wealth I have concealed this, my last Will and Testament, to bear witness that it is not fit for men of understanding to be dazzled by mere glitter. Riches are but borrowed conveniences to be repaid to our successors, and while all the pleasures of this world are delightful, none are eternal.

This letter is the treasure of my treasure, being a thing of much more real use than all the gems and precious metals heaped beside it. Here I have abridged thirteen rules of conduct proper to the behaviour of kings. Wise indeed will be the Prince of Power who regulates himself to act in accordance with the admonitions which I hereby declare:

I Never dismiss any servant at the request of other persons. For anyone who is close to a king will always unwittingly arouse jealousy and envy among those who do not enjoy such happiness. And when they see that a king develops any affection for such a servant, they will not cease, by a thousand calumnies, to undermine his position and render him odious to his master.

II Always preserve your ministers, counsellors, and grandees in a balance of mutual understanding with one another, that they may unanimously labour for the good of the state.

III Never trust to the submissions of enemies. The more affection they display and the louder their protesta-tions of service, the more they are to be distrusted. There is no relying upon the friendship of an enemy. Like the siren who charms with the intent to destroy, an enemy who approaches with the countenance of a friend is to be shunned.

IV Preserve carefully that which has been diligently sought after and acquired, for we do not have every day the same opportunity to gain what we desire. When we have not preserved that which we once acquired, we are left with only the vexation of having lost it. We cannot fetch back the flown arrow even if we should eat our fingers for madness.

V Never be too hasty in business. Before executing any enterprise, it behooves one to weigh and examine in detail one's strategy. Things done rashly come fre-quently to a mischievous conclusion. He repents in vain who cannot recall what he has done amiss.

VI Never despise good counsel and prudence. If it is nec-essary for a king to make peace with his enemies in order to deliver himself out of their hands, let him do it without delay.

VII *Avoid the company of dissemblers and never hearken to their smooth speeches. Their bosoms carry nothing but the seeds of enmity, and can never bring forth the fruits of friendship.*

VIII *Always be merciful. Never punish a subject or servant for faults committed through infirmity. Consider the weakness of all men, and in charity and goodness suffer their defects. Subjects have always committed faults, and kings have always pardoned them when they have been guilty only of the common frailties of human nature.*

IX *Never procure the harm or injury of any person. If you do good, good will be done to you; but if you do evil, the same will be measured back to you again.*

X *Never seek after any thing which may be unworthy of you or contrary to your nature. There are too many persons who abandon their own affairs to intrude into other people's business, and finish by doing nothing at all. The crow who attempted to learn to fly like a partridge, a way of flying impossible to him, forgot his own skill and crashed to the ground.*

XI *Be of a mild and affable temper. Mildness in society is like salt in our food; as salt seasons and gives relish, so mildness gives contentment to everyone. The sword of steel is less sharp than the sword of mildness, for it vanquishes even invincible armies.*

XII *Seek out faithful ministers and never admit knaves and deceivers into your service or councils. By wise and honest ministers the kingdom will be kept safe, and the king's secrets never revealed.*

XIII Never be disturbed by the accidents of the world. A man of resolution and true courage suffers all adversities with a settled fortitude. Rely upon the providence of Heaven. It is the fool who minds nothing but his pastime and his pleasure.

Several fables exist which illustrate and explain these admonitions, and if King Dabschelim will hear them, he must apply to the Merciful Physician, wherever he may be. Know that the man called Bidpai is the storehouse of these stories; they will answer as from an oracle of Heaven every question that can enter The King's heart concerning the happiness of his people. So be it.

Houschenk, King of the Past."

Dr. Bidpai

My wife was nervous and skittish as she helped pin me
into the full Brahminical regalia. "But why," she insisted, "must you see The King? What can he do to
help you and your students?"

I stood poised like some peculiar statue in the dance
of life, arms extended and practising a proper look of
ceremonial disdain while she tucked and tugged the
cloth into neat folds around my body. She was not
alone in feeling this flurry of domestic apprehension.
Her instincts were entirely correct: I was terrified. Yet
in no way should I show anything except supreme
confidence.

"Now, now, my dear," I said in the most imperious
tone I could muster, "there's no need to fret. None
whatsoever." I knew such male arrogance would give
her the blind strength of anger and that, at least, was
better than the helplessness of fear. The fear was mine
to swallow.

"I just wish to have a brief word in His Majesty's ear
about a certain situation," I continued. "That's all. He
may be able to act in such a way as to benefit everybody."

"He may also neatly remove your head from your shoulders before sunset and then destroy your entire family, including every cousin of a cousin," she muttered, with her mouth half full of ornamental pins. She jabbed vigorously at a fold of silk that was pinched between her fingers, then knelt back on her heels to survey the effect, brushing the cloth smooth in no gentle manner. "His Highness is hardly famous for his kindness," she said testily, snatching the pins from between her lips, never looking in my face. "How will a meddling old priest reform him now? Have there not been enough deaths already? Are not the jails full of men and women who have merely irritated The King? What can you do that's so different?"

She was right, of course, and there was no answer to any of this. I breathed deeply and said nothing. Soon she would run herself down and remain grudgingly content with the knowledge that whatever happened, at least she had "told me so."

"There," she said, standing up and stepping well back for a final inspection. "That's about it."

I lowered my arms and went to her. Our eyes met, and for a moment I thought she would accept no appeasement. But she let me give her the hug.

"Don't worry," I said, when she was in my arms. "It will be all right. I promise."

"That's enough," she said crisply, and pushed me away. "You'll muss yourself up." She patted out some new creases by my shoulders. "You'd better be going, or you'll be late," she said, and gave me that wry smile which fond wives reserve for stubborn husbands.

I slipped on my best sandals and went down to the street. The usual medley of midmorning sounds leapt to my ears: children shouted, men with handcarts yelled, women with loads on their heads bustled and chattered, passing bullock carts heaped high with firewood rattled and creaked. Hagglers, loungers, sellers, beggars, thieves, and sadhus completed the raucous bustle of human activity teeming in this city thoroughfare.

My eyes met those of three of my students waiting in a nearby doorway. Their smiles were sudden and genuine. One of them exclaimed loudly how marvellous I looked and other such reassuring courtesies. But the eldest remarked with more ironic accuracy that my outfit was "quite stylish for a man intending to swim with a crocodile."

"In any case," he said, "we'd like to accompany you to the palace, if you don't mind."

Of course I didn't, so we set off, shouldering our way through the throng. Or, to be precise, they shouldered and I followed closely in their wake—a lucky old man, I suppose, to have even one student left after the lambasting I'd delivered the night before. It wasn't luck, though, I realized a moment later, but faded ferocity: I'd *meant* to shake off the whole crew.

"I am unwilling to go down in history as the weak-kneed philosopher Bidpai, who did nothing to try to inhibit the atrocities committed by the tyrant Dabschelim," I had said. At least twenty mouths around the room dropped open with a collective gasp; never in all my years of teaching the ritual observances, the old stories, the chants and spells of tradition, had I ever expressed a single political opinion. Now here I was suddenly preaching treason and sedition. You can bet it sent a shiver down their spines, which is exactly what I intended.

I don't remember my remaining words in detail, but it felt right saying them. It was as if the will to fight suddenly possessed my body, spurring me forward in a vigorous rush. I soared on wings of inspiration like an eagle in an updraft. I could see fear jump into their rabbit eyes as my argument sped away. Oh, yes, in their view I was quite mad; no one could deny it. So what about these diehards leading me through the crowds? Either they were three mental defectives lacking any sense of self-preservation, or else the Great Provider was humouring me through my last moments with the luxury of youthful companionship. What did it matter? I never reject what is offered.

"Aleee . . . it's Dr. Bidpai and his assistants on their way to cure The King of naughtiness!" a young smiling sadhu jeered. There was a brief hesitation as dozens of eyes flickered between us and the beaming sadhu. Anyone actually noticing my immaculate costume confirmed in a flash: "Yes, he *is* off to see The King! How strange!" Some, like the sadhu, obviously knew about my speech the night before. A few women began to giggle openly.

"Well, good luck to you, Dr. Bidpai," the sadhu cried. "Good luck to you in this life and the one immediately following." Laughter broke out here and there and rippled up and down the street. I myself joined in and waved my arms about to acknowledge the fun, but my students were afraid and closed ranks like cornered wolves, their expressions grim.

"Keep moving, you fools," I hissed and poked them each in the back with stiffened fingers. The crowd laughed as we moved on. The absurdity of the scene that would soon transpire—when I, as it were, put my head into the lion's jaws—brought tears of delight to all eyes. And I entirely agreed with their sentiment. Nevertheless, it was not long before I found myself following the chamberlain down a long, cool corridor in the palace to my appointment with the king.

I bowed when I was announced to his presence, but said nothing. His Majesty was reclining casually upon a dazzle of brightly coloured cushions strewn about on a raised dais of

teak and ivory. He was speaking to some courtiers, and there was an atmosphere of frivolity about the place, as if a party were being planned.

"Oh, and Menlipses—" beckoned the king. His eyes brushed me and his lips stretched into a wide smile.

"Sire?" responded this dainty fop with a jutting chin. He slid neatly forward onto one foot, almost a heron's pose, with arms curved out from his torso and hands upswept like little wingtips, neck and beard craned forward into the fullest curve of hovering obeisance. You could hear his eyelashes flap.

"See to it that we invite Kurkshar," continued the king. "His new wife is so very luscious. Seat her on my right and put him well away on the left, so that you can divert him personally with your clownish chatter."

"It shall be done, O Magnificent One," said the hovering one with a peculiar twisting nod. "Is there anything else, Sire?"

"No, that will do, Menlipses, thank you." The king's face turned slowly until his eyes and smile fixed on me. Menlipses drew himself gracefully upright and then elegantly minced out of sight to begin arranging whatever he had to arrange.

"And now for you, Dr. Bidpai," began the king. "We have never met, but, of course, who has not heard of you? Such a distinguished scholar of our heritage, born into the highest-ranking Brahminic family, an expert, so we hear tell, on many arcane traditions from deep in our glorious past. . . . Oh, indeed, how very interesting! Now tell me. To what do we owe this unexpected pleasure? Do you need money for some worthy project? Or do you solicit my assistance for some special cause? Come, tell me! What is it you want?"

Normally I am hardly shy, but something warned me on this occasion to hold back just a bit longer. It was all a question of timing. I grinned at Dabschelim like some confident old fool too stupid to harbour fear. Our eyes locked gently and I saw his pupils flare before he sighed a more amiable smile that briefly melted the imperial gaze. It was a beginning, and putting palms together before my face, I bowed.

"Well, your silence is quite delightful and rare," the king said. "How amazing to meet a greybeard who doesn't immediately begin to spout gloom and doom unless I undertake *his* such-and-such pet panacea. I am the constant recipient of endless free advice regarding the methods of our salvation. Oh, I try and listen but it's usually so very long-winded and boring . . . as much as a king can do to keep awake these days. So if I do catch myself yawning and nodding off in the middle of some fervent exhortation, I simply conclude that the fool can't know what he's talking about. At least he could keep *me* awake—the one person possibly able to help him achieve his aims! It is absolutely unbelievable how boring people become as soon as they believe their own speeches. There's no fun to life if everything becomes so deadly earnest and serious. No— I'll have none of it, thank you. Nowadays, as you may have heard, it amuses me to clap obsessives into jail rather suddenly. I understand my dungeons are positively bulging with these dreary meddlers, but at least my audience chamber is uncontaminated by their cranky theorizings, and a greater proportion of normal people can go about their business!

"I am rather eating my own words, though, aren't I, Dr. Bidpai? Going on and on like this. But I appreciate the subtlety of your approach. It's most unusual that anyone lets me talk. Come, come, now, Dr. Bidpai—I shan't bite you. Speak out, please, and tell us why you have kept so extraordinarily quiet for so long."

"Your Majesty," I said, "my silence stems from the respect and deference which are naturally due to kings, especially one raised so high in rank by virtue of power uniquely combined with sensitivity." This careful wording appeared to increase the king's pleasure, and with a relaxed smile he folded his hands behind his head and lay back even more comfortably upon his dazzling cushions. I made another bow of courtesy and continued.

"Speech, as Your Royal Highness has already suggested, exposes the speaker to risk. Once upon a time the kings of China, India, Persia, and Greece were all together and each agreed to deliver a saying which might be recorded to their posterity. The King of China said: 'I have more power over what I do not speak than I have over what escapes my lips.'

"The King of Persia: 'A man's own tongue may cut his throat.'

"The King of India: 'I am the slave of what I have spoken, but the master of what I conceal.'

"The King of Greece: 'I have never regretted imposing silence upon myself, but have often repented the uttering of words.'

"So, Sire, if speech is so universally regarded as a

reliable instrument for man's downfall, then it must follow that the antidote is deliberate silence. I have pursued this policy since entering this chamber with the results Your Highness can witness. Although I now prattle under your direct command, it is best that I again revert to the safety of silence rather than risk the rewards of Your Majesty's displeasure."

I bowed again and for a brief moment thought I had overdone it. The king seemed stunned, eyes staring, mouth slightly open, his breathing shallow as if in a light trance. But he came back as quickly and vigorously as I'd guessed he might, shook himself upright and with a huge, uninhibited smile of delight, clapped his hands and called out:

"Bravo, Dr. Bidpai, bravo! Well said! You need have no fear of boring me! I shall listen carefully to whatever you have to say. Please continue. I grant you complete freedom of speech. Dispense with the niceties: say what you really have to say."

King Dabschelim's happiness infected even some of the Palace Guard who, although standing rigidly to attention with eyes dead ahead, displayed the very slightest softening of their military grimness by imperceptibly relaxing their lips, transforming their normal down-mouth fearsomeness into a distinctly more horizontal line of pleasure that was probably the closest they ever came to a smile while on duty. Elsewhere in the chamber, idle courtiers and sundry dignitaries caught the king's mood more openly. Spontaneous delight erupted about me in innumerable wide, even toothy, smiles, the odd cheer or two, and even an outright burst of polite applause in mimicry of the king. I gathered the not unpleasant impression that invisible doors into an especially select club had miraculously swung open to welcome its newest luminary—me! It was anyone's guess how long this incredible situation would endure; I plunged ahead.

"Your Majesty is more than gracious to an old man who appears empty-handed before you. Yet because I seek neither money nor anyone's daughter in marriage, I can afford to speak some truth. At my age one has nothing to lose. Sire, do with me as you will, but what I have to say must be said and soon. Since no one else is saying it, the responsibility to do so, much as I may personally regret the inconvenience, appears to have fallen on me! I begin to bore even myself, however, with these cautious preliminaries. And boring either you or myself, Your Majesty, is something I am distinctly determined to avoid."

Carefully and gently I began, much as a swimmer slowly dips his toes into a cold mountain stream before jumping in. I spoke of the greatness achieved by Dabschelim's ancestors, named those great kings of yesteryear who had scored legendary victories and established bright reigns of unimpaired honour. I employed my words as both narcotic and scalpel, weaving a trance of reassurance before dancing in quickly to lance the skin of fixed notions with a razor-sharp criticism delivered under such an entertaining camouflage that, for a while at least, no one could be sure whether my manner was serious, humorous, or insanely insulting. The words took me and delivered themselves. I was merely the actor, the spout of a kettle steaming out inspiration. Having painted a glorious picture of our past, I then, by degrees, contrasted it with the present bleakness and the even bleaker prospects ahead.

Dabschelim sat watching me carefully, gently squeezing the sides of his nose. My words had bite, but at this stage never lacked courtesy. I quoted in part my speech to the students the night before, and even used the phrase "odious tyranny." Still the king held silence, probably because he remained suspended in a state of disbelief. Immediately after any verbal cut my words would glide back into flattery and compliment, their meaning always nudging the edge of uncertainty. His Highness began to frown and fidget. You could feel tension suffusing the chamber. People grew too embarrassed to watch me and stared at the floor.

My voice soared on and on. Oh, it was fun: there is no denying that. At the same time it was sad, so unnecessary, so . . . what? So unoriginal? So repetitious? It had already been done so much better so many times before that I felt myself dead to caring, dead to the world. Out of the corner of my eye I watched myself play the fool. Oh, I was good at it, all right!

The king's face is reddening, his expression fiercer; he's going to burst, he's standing up, the time is now! I stabbed deep with my final message, plunging in all the way, full pelt, damn the consequences.

"Does it bore you then, Sire, to know that although you can peer at stars easily from your magnificent observatory, you remain blind to the suffering right in front of your nose? Are you a king or some kind of melon? Is something the matter with your brain or your eyes?"

The king leapt to his feet.

"*Guards!*" he roared. "Seize this fool! Off with his head immediately! Lop it from his shoulders with the sharpest sword! *Now!* Kill him! Kill the maniac!"

I breathed deeply and slowly exhaled. The Captain of the Guard was unsheathing his sword and running towards me. From behind, another guard locked my arms in a violent grip. Uniforms surrounded me. I was punched, kicked, shoved, pushed and leaned on until I stumbled forward onto my knees. The sword flashed upward. "Goodbye for now," I coughed out feebly.

"*Halt!*" rang out the king's voice. The scene froze as if set in amber. I felt my breath coming in . . . going out. The sword was lowered. My body was yanked upright. There was blood on my face, on my robe. Everything ached.

"Take this geriatric nincompoop away," Dabschelim said, and struck his forehead a glancing blow with the base of his palm. "Stuff him into the foulest hole on bread and water! Give him nothing but the worst! Drop him down that toilet of a bottle dungeon! Get him out of my sight!" His Majesty turned and stomped out of the chamber. To say he exited in a huff would be an excess of understatement.

I was catapulted down corridor after corridor to reach the stinking mouth of the bottle dungeon. They shoved me over the edge. Only the putrid accumulation of ordure at the bottom saved me from breaking my back. The stench consumed me; I fainted in my own vomit.

CONVERGENCE

The scene was quite different when Dr. Bidpai and
King Dabschelim met again. Ever since he had heard
King Houschenk's letter, Dabschelim had experienced
a breathless agony of spirit which would only be truly
abated by sight of the Merciful Physician himself. All
the way back from the mountains his breast kindled
with fragile hope as if a tiny sweet-voiced bird sang in
the secret garden of his heart. He hardly dared to think
on it, lest crude rationality blow out the spark, causing
the bird to fly. Oh, he knew what a fool of a king he was
now: of that there could be no doubt. "A man comes to
me," he mused over and over again, "who is neither
crank nor flatterer, a man who can speak sense and
properly diagnose my condition, no mere tonguester,
ambitious for himself, but someone capable of good
advice, someone who cares, someone who cares for me,
who cares for all of us . . . and what do I do? I get angry.
I cannot listen. I label him a dealer in frivolous dis-
course. I almost kill him. Then I cast him into a dungeon and have probably killed him anyway. Oh, oh,
oh . . ."

It is not possible to describe these inner sighs of hope-lessness which overcame the king from time to time on his dash back to the palace. He and his party rode on and on without stopping for rest. No one remarked upon it, but more than once Dabschelim's strength faltered and bitter tears of regret, even disconsolate sobs, were silently plucked away from his face by the rushing wind. "Oh, if only we are not too late," he said to himself again and again. "If only we are not too late."

They were not too late. The two young horsemen whom Dabschelim had dispatched in advance of his own group arrived more than a day before him and secured Bidpai's immediate release. Despite nearly twenty days of incarceration, the old man was alive, even radiant. The king's servants who were com-manded to administer to Bidpai's every need failed to comprehend his high spirits. His body was still bruised in many places, he limped because a costume pin had pierced his thigh during his fall into the dungeon, and his face . . . his face was gaunt and papery as if his lips might suddenly start to tear apart at the corners if he smiled. And he did smile. His sunken eyes were so bright and intense that the king's attendants, strip-ping and bathing him, pampering every inch of his skin with soothing oils and unguents, hardly dared to meet his gaze. Bidpai did most of the talking. He needed to, as part of his sudden reintroduction to the company of others. After his confinement, the society of people and their sheer bodily closeness seemed to wash over him in waves of profound relief. Relaxed, he babbled on.

Apparently, after regaining consciousness, he had

managed to haul himself to the dungeon's perimeter, where the ceiling sloped down to the floor and the filth was less vile. He slowly unwound his robe, tore off a square to sit upon and began to nurse himself as best he could. Luckily no bones were broken. He drank hardly any of his daily water ration, but instead wet strips of his robe from the lowered jug and spent hours wiping and washing himself. His entire routine centred on keeping clean and calm. Cleanliness became the obsessive mainstay of his aloneness. For hours he would squeeze and massage the stab wound in his thigh, trying, despite the pain, to keep the area supple and loose. He neatly bandaged cuts and abrasions with longer, cleaned-up strips from his robe, sucking these minor wounds clean beforehand, wherever possible, of any foul festerings of old blood, scab, or pus. When all these slow and delicate ablutions were complete for the day, he would throw himself into a light trance, sitting comfortably on his square of cloth—letting his mind follow the even surge of his breath. This meditation allowed a hypnotic passage away from immediacy to other realms of nourishment, and since, overall, he felt like one huge tingling bruise squatting there in the dark, it is hardly to be wondered that he travelled frequently in this manner.

"There, there—you're all right now," said Dabschelim's personal physician as he concluded his detailed medical examination. "In fact, you're in remarkably good condition for a man of your age. Sun and fresh air, some food and a little walking to exercise that leg of yours, and you'll be back to normal in no time at all!

Now look here, Dr. Bidpai, the king has sent strict orders that we are to pamper you with every conceivable luxury pending his arrival. If there's anything you require—anything at all—please do not hesitate to ask for it. These apartments have been especially opened for your comfortable recovery, and every service of the palace is at your disposal. We are expecting the king to arrive sometime in the next day or so, and I understand he is very anxious to speak with you. In the meantime we hope you will enjoy your stay with us and I am sure I speak for all the staff when I say how delighted we are to be able to pronounce your name in public once again. Welcome back, Dr. Bidpai, welcome back! Oh, yes . . . I almost forgot . . . your wife . . . your wife, sir, has been informed of your change in fortune and is being escorted here at this very moment. I hope this little reunion meets with your approval and suspect that now is the time for my colleagues and me to retire so that you may rest in privacy. Whenever you want anything, simply clap your hands.''

So completely slick and effective was this man's bedside manner that Bidpai only just recovered in time to mumble a startled, feeble, "Thank you . . . thank you very much," before all the attendants seemed to bow and melt away, and he found himself alone again, albeit in rather changed circumstances. He was just beginning to observe his new, plush surroundings, noting the abundance of cushions everywhere and the soft thickness of their textures, when his wife appeared. Their meeting began exactly as one might have expected in view of the situation.

"My God, but you look dreadful," she said in her inimitable way. "What's wrong with your skin? It looks all greasy." She stepped closer, arms akimbo, peering at him as if he were a suspected piece of rotten fruit.

"Some rather charming young women have just given me a full body massage," Bidpai said. "I believe it's part of normal prisoner reinstatement policy. Anyway, how are you? Have you had much bother while I've been away?"

"No, no bother aside from worrying myself half to death. I told you this would come to no good. Why can't you ever listen? Some of your students have even been hiding out in the hills, terrified for their very lives."

"Oh, I am sorry to hear that! Well, never mind. It's all over now; you'll see. Why don't we just enjoy this place?" He took her hand casually and after only a tiny pause of reluctance, she came with him to the balcony, which overlooked Dabschelim's magnificent palace gardens. They spent that and the next day relaxing in each other's company.

King Dabschelim arrived the following evening, tense, exhausted, and filthy from his hard ride. As soon as he learned that Bidpai was alive and well, a deep sense of relief swept through his mind. He refreshed himself in his baths and, after a light meal, went straight to bed and slept without any trace of his usual insomnia. When he arose very late the next morning, he felt calm and in balance. He sent for Bidpai at around three o'clock in the afternoon.

Dabschelim was waiting in his easy chair by a table,

but all the astronomical instruments—callipers, protractors, and whatnot—had been shoved to one side to
accommodate a handsome lacquered tray placed
within easy reach. On the tray stood a yellow tureen
filled with pink sherbet topped with crushed nuts. A
pair of choice glass goblets matched two fine golden
spoons, and strewn around the base of the tureen, indeed covering the whole remaining surface of the tray,
were the scattered blossoms of the most delicate pale
red roses. These tender petals subtly dispersed an exquisite aura of sweetness throughout the room that
even surpassed their fragile perfume.

"Will you share a bowl of sherbet with me?" the king
asked Bidpai with a smile. "I always find it such a treat
to freshen the mouth before one talks."

"Oh, yes, please," answered Bidpai. "I would like
that."

Dabschelim reached for the golden ladle that hung
by its handle over the tureen's rim and scooped out two
hearty portions of the cold delicacy. He served Bidpai
with his own hands. They ate in silence for a few moments, and then the king proceeded to give Bidpai a
conducted tour of his observatory.

"You've heard of this place, of course," the king said.
"I seem to remember your mentioning it the first time
we met," he added with a smile.

Bidpai smiled back but said nothing.

"Well this is Dabschelim's Folly, then," the king
said with a sweep of his spoon. He scooped up another
mouthful of sherbet from his goblet and then, pacing
up and down, told Bidpai some of the observatory's

history and function. It was not long before he pulled out a few of his favourite star maps from their ebony cannisters and unrolled them to explain certain subtle points of astronomical observation. And, to be sure, Bidpai was very interested in all that Dabschelim had to say.

But Dabschelim interrupted himself, drew up a chair and bade Bidpai sit down next to him, "Because," he said, "much more has happened in this room recently than I can quite believe. The star maps are delightful, of course, but only scratch the surface of my story. It's beginning to stitch together in my head now, but I'm afraid you're a key thread to the patchwork of my understanding. If you don't mind, I'd like to tell you about my recent dream which, strangely enough, was set in this very room. Would you care for some more sherbet?"

"No, thank you, Your Majesty. Not for the moment, if you don't mind. Tell me, Sire, what was in your dream?"

"A shooting star," answered the king, "and the moon . . . and a man in green . . ." And he proceeded to tell Bidpai all about that vivid night that seemed so far away and yet so very near.

"Wonderful," exclaimed Bidpai, when the king had finished.

"Yes," said the king. "Now perhaps you'll begin to understand me when I say that this scene is where the seen converges on the unseen."

Bidpai smiled politely at the royal display of wit. "What happened next?" he asked. "I know you left

suddenly for Zindawar; the horsemen you sent ahead
with orders for my release informed us of that fact. But
they said they were forbidden to speak of what tran-
spired in the mountains."

"Yes, that's true. I wanted to surprise you myself,
you see. I wanted you to be the first to know."

"Did you find a treasure, then, Sire?"

"Yes, indeed I did, and you shall hear all. But before
we get to that I would like to hear something from you.
You see, it was only two weeks or so after you came to
see me that I had my dream. I'm sure the events are
related, but I think what's particularly relevant is
what you came to say to me. I freely admit to having
completely forgotten you and your message until one
particular event in the mountains seared your name
forever in my memory. What I am saying is this: you
came to criticize my statecraft. At the time I was inca-
pable of listening, as you are unlikely to forget. Now,
however, I want to listen to you. Therefore, can you
please repeat everything you said that day?"

"I think I'll have a bit more sherbet now, if you don't
mind, Your Majesty."

"Yes, yes—of course, Dr. Bidpai. Take your time.
When you're ready . . . I'll wait . . . ."

And so after a few more cooling spoonfuls of pink
sherbet, Bidpai began to repeat what he had said before. The form of his presentation was altered to suit
these friendlier circumstances, but the content of his
message was the same. It did not lack punch or bite. He
said what had to be said about Dabschelim's manner
of living and the need for reform in his behaviour and

government. The king listened with the greatest attention and never once interrupted the old man and, when Bidpai was finished, Dabschelim said that everything he had heard had made a tremendous impact upon his mind. They were both silent for a few moments, looking at one another. The king smiled gently, relieved in spite of the pain of the occasion.

"Shall we have some tea? I think that would be nice, don't you?" said the king, scratching his chin with a bejewelled forefinger. He clapped his hands and a retainer appeared.

"I rarely visit this room during daylight," the king remarked after a pause. "It's really rather pleasant."

"Yes, it is, Sire," Bidpai responded. "I particularly enjoy the filigree window screens," he said, pointing to some white marble carvings screening the palace gardens and the Royal Bedchamber. "They're almost like lace, aren't they? Unbelievable workmanship when you think about it. They give the observatory such a soft atmosphere."

"Yes," said the king. "Stone as delicate as lace. It *is* lovely!"

The tea arrived, and once again the king personally served Bidpai his refreshment. Then, after only a single sip from his own cup, he rummaged in the folds of his robe and extracted two documents, one being King Houschenk's original letter and the other Farsi's meticulously copied-out translation.

"Now let me tell you about the treasure," the king said. And he did. And when that story was done he showed the letters to Bidpai, and pointed out each of their names in the satin document from long ago.

"That's quite amazing," said Bidpai. "I'm sure I cannot explain it."

"But do you know the stories that are mentioned here, the ones which illustrate King Houschenk's admonitions?"

"Yes, I do," answered Bidpai. "They were given to me to memorize a long time ago, although at the time I had no idea why."

"What's this reference to the Merciful Physician mean?"

"Well, I'm not sure, but I can tell you this: when I was given these stories as a young man—also in the mountains, I might add, near Toxila—I was told to remember that they were a type of medicine and not to be taken lightly."

"Would you please tell me one? Could we start with the first of Houschenk's precepts? You know, the one that reads . . ." Dabschelim fumbled for a moment with the documents in his lap. "Ah, yes—here it is.'Never dismiss any servant at the request of other persons. For anyone who is close to a king will always unwittingly arouse jealousy and envy among those who do not enjoy such happiness. And when they see that a king develops any affection for such a servant, they will not cease, by a thousand calumnies, to undermine his position and render him odious to his master.' "

"Oh, yes—that's easy," said Bidpai. He shifted in his

seat to ease the pressure on his still painful thigh. "That's the story known as 'Kalila and Dimna' or, as it's sometimes called, 'How to Lose Friends.' I'll tell it to you if you like, but it's quite long and will certainly take up the rest of the day and most of the night. You'll need to keep me topped up with tea and water, or my voice will surely give out."

"Oh, don't worry about that," said the king. "We can take care of you. I have a feeling you're going to be a rather pampered storyteller."

"Easy does it, please, Your Highness. I have a low requirement for luxury, although I'll admit preferring to avoid any more bottle dungeons for a while."

They both laughed at this reminder of their recent topsy-turvy world where things changed and changed again in an invisible pattern.

"One question before I begin, please, Your Majesty," Bidpai said.

"Yes, yes. What is it?"

"What happened to the treasure, to Farsi, and the hermit? I'm curious to know."

"Well, I'll tell you in detail another time," replied the king, "but here's the gist of it. Everyone who was there, including the blacksmith and all my men, was allowed to approach the treasure once and carry away all he could hold on his person. Only the old hermit declined. He said he'd lived so long without wealth but with happiness that he didn't want to risk a reversal now. Peculiar fellow, really, but very interesting nevertheless. Anyway, these withdrawals, as you may well imagine, hardly made a dent in that pile of riches.

Next I gave a couple of chests of gold to the town of Zindawar so they could build a hospital or a school or some community project; told the city elders to sort it out among themselves and that I would return in a few years to see what they had accomplished. Then I saw Farsi . . . dear old Farsi. He's such an amusing man and so very, very bright. Well, I thought, why not build a school for languages right there, on the spot where it all happened? To Farsi, then, I gave away another four or five chests—diamonds mostly—and asked him to found a university dedicated to the study of languages old and new, and the preservation of human heritage in revitalized forms. That's about it. The rest of the treasure coffers are on their way back here now. Some of the local Zindawar militia boys are escorting it, together with a few of the officers who originally travelled with me. What I'm going to do with it I don't know, but somehow I'm sure your influence will enter into the final picture. Now please, Dr. Bidpai, will you begin that first story? What's it called again?"

" 'Kalila and Dimna,' Your Majesty, and here's how it goes." Bidpai took a long sip of his lukewarm tea and began.

KALILA AND DIMNA

One day a merchant from Distawand set out on a journey. He travelled with his servants in a cart drawn by two bulls named Schanzabeh and Bandabeh. Soon they came to a section of road which was so muddy that Schanzabeh sank down to his belly. The merchant, his servants, and Bandabeh tried to haul Schanzabeh out but they couldn't budge him.

Impatient at the delay, the merchant decided to continue his journey with only Bandabeh pulling the cart. He left one of his servants behind with Schanzabeh, hoping that if the road dried out, they would follow later. But after spending one night near the bull, the servant grew bored with waiting in what seemed a hopeless situation. So he left and rejoined his master, telling him that Schanzabeh had died.

Meanwhile, Schanzabeh managed to free himself from the mud, and wandered off to seek pasture. After days of rambling he emerged from some wooded hills into a green and solitary valley where the grass grew long and sweet and a lazy river flowed by pools of cool, clear water. Schanzabeh stayed in this valley and ate and drank his fill until he became quite fat.

But Schanzabeh was alone. No other bull or cow
kept him company, and frequently and mournfully he
bellowed out his loneliness in terrible sounds that
echoed up and down the valley. The lion who ruled all
the wild animals of the nearby forest had never heard
anything like it. He ordered a wild boar to go and see
what strange new creature was making this dreadful
racket. The boar crashed through thickets, briars,
thorns, and brambles until he came upon Schanzabeh
drinking from the river. When he beheld such a huge
beast with sharp horns, he froze among the bankside
reeds in wide-eyed amazement. Meanwhile Schanzabeh, unaware of his observer, raised his head from the
water and roared forth three or four horrible bellows,
so shocking the poor boar that he tumbled backwards
into some deep and gooey mud.

Later when he made his way back to the lion, the
boar told all he had seen of the terrible beast, and his
report convinced the lion that it was best to repair to
his den. Of course, the king's den was fairly sumptu-
ous, located in a scattered grove about halfway up and
right into the north side of the valley, enlarged over
generations from a vast open cave mouth that gradually funnelled back into the gently sloping limestone.
Under the protective overhang of its entrance, on a
slightly convex arena known to all the animals simply
as the Tongue, the lion conducted daily sessions of his
court. These were informal morning meetings, open to
anyone, where creatures gave voice to their grievances
and woes, one against another, seeking the king's rul-
ing; discussed any news—good or bad—and employed

relevant information to amend, devise, reform, and re-interpret the various institutions of the state. Situated farther back, off the first sharp branching to the left, about twenty feet into the cave itself, was the Royal Lair, dry and warm, with its main reception chamber even having a small natural window eroded out of the parallel hillside. It was to this bright and airy sanctuary that the lion commanded his food to be brought every day. He remained there for some time, enjoying the view across the valley from his little window, and only appearing in public for the daily sessions of his court.

Now it happened that among the lion's attendants were two jackal brothers named Kalila and Dimna, who were both very clever and cunning. 'I wonder why the lion never leaves his den?' Dimna asked his brother one morning, when they were lounging about in the sun. 'Don't you think it strange that he no longer goes out prowling and hunting?'

'If I were you, brother,' said Kalila, 'I would contain my curiosity on such matters. We are the lion's servants, and our business is to wait upon him and obey his commands—not to pry into his affairs.'

'Yes, but have you not heard how short-tempered he is these days? Apparently anyone who asks him a question gets a gruff and impatient reply. He always seems to be sour and cross, and will hardly allow anyone to speak with him. Maybe it's because he is frightened that the huge beast in the meadow will conquer his kingdom.'

'Are you out of your mind or simply tired of living?'

Kalila replied quickly. 'If you don't watch out, you'll get exactly what you deserve. Do I have to tell you how dangerous it is to meddle in The King's business? You remind me of the story of the monkey who tried his hand at something he didn't understand.'

The Carpenter's Monkey

'One morning a carpenter's pet monkey watched his master splitting logs. The man sat on a log and pounded wedges into each end with a heavy mallet, causing it to split slightly open along its length. Then he stood up and whacked each wedge several times with a sledgehammer until the log broke in two. After several hours of this activity, he grew tired and went off to eat lunch. The monkey was very curious, and wanted to try log-splitting too. Here was his chance, for the carpenter had left behind a log which was only partially split—the two wedges still being in position. He sat on the log, imitating the man. The mallet was so heavy he needed two hands to lift it over his head, and even then he was thrown off balance. He hit the wedge a clumsy, sideways blow, knocking it out so that the split suddenly closed on his balls. The monkey let out an awful screech and his eyes almost popped from their sockets. He screamed and he screamed, and when the carpenter ran up and saw what his stupid pet had done, he boxed its ears so furiously that the poor little monkey finally fainted from shock.'

Appeal to the active imagination cancels the need for "reason or explanation."

Karel Reisz (quoting Eisenstein)

49

'I've heard that story before,' Dimna said. 'And it mainly applies to those who have no idea how to accomplish things. It is also true that if you risk nothing, you achieve nothing, for fortune favours the bold. I am interested in the lion because I think I may be able to help him. And if I can help him, then I am sure to be rewarded.'

'Come, come, dear brother!' Kalila laughed. 'How are you going to help The King? He barely speaks to you, let alone listens to your advice.'

'My first step is to obtain an audience with the lion. Later I shall ask him indirectly what he thinks about that creature in the meadow. I am confident I can phrase this question in such a way as not to irritate him. Anyway, I understand that so far none of his ministers has dared even mention the subject, and it is obviously troubling him.'

'Kings seldom choose the best creatures to act as their ministers,' said Kalila. 'Often it is simply the one who happens to be nearby who becomes a favourite, much as a vine attaches itself to the nearest tree.'

'That's exactly my point,' said Dimna. 'As I see it, this is my chance to present myself at court and test my native wit and cunning. Certainly many of The King's present advisers are stupider and more cowardly than I. If fortune sees fit to favour such dolts, why should she not also favour me? There are many paths to greatness. Some achieve it through virtue, some through strength, some through service, and some through cleverness in seizing opportunity.'

'Be that as it may,' Kalila said, 'I think you will

meet more trouble than you expect. You are gambling that the lion will take a liking to you, and help you achieve your ambitions. But kings are notoriously fickle: one moment they will be all smiles and make you imagine you are much loved, then suddenly seem not to know you, or, even worse, to hate you. You are exposing yourself to a wind which can blow equally strongly in opposite directions. However, I can see you are determined to go, whatever I say, so all I can do, brother, is to wish you good luck.'

Dimna said goodbye to Kalila and went immediately to the Tongue to present himself to the lion. Once he was announced at court, the king bade him approach to state his business.

'May it please Your Majesty,' Dimna said, 'I have come to offer my slender capacities to Your Majesty's service. Please condescend to use me in whatever way Your Majesty sees fit, for even a little toothpick proves a comfort to the greatest king when food sticks between his teeth.'

The lion was as astonished as he was pleased at these unexpected words, and immediately formed a good opinion of Dimna.

'Well spoken, jackal,' he said. 'You have stepped boldly yet respectfully forward, and deserve the trial which you request. You are welcome to this court and to our presence.'

And from that time onward Dimna increasingly enjoyed the lion's company. They spent many hours together in private conversations covering a multitude of subjects. Early one day, when the moment seemed appropriate, Dimna asked the lion why he never ventured forth from his den. They were chatting easily in the king's main reception room, both squatting on their haunches. From the window Dimna and the lion gazed through a fringe of sun-impacted trees right down across the meadowlands and the river to the other side of the valley. It was always a spectacular view, and today the mood was especially calm.

'Your Majesty,' the jackal said, 'you once took great pleasure in walking, hunting, and sporting about the kingdom. There was a bounce in your step and vigour in your roar, and you were seen everywhere. For several weeks now, however, Your Majesty has kept himself cooped up at court—usually secluded in the privacy of the Royal Lair. Surely there is a cause for such a change in behaviour, and I, for one, wish you would confide in me if something is troubling you. After all, what are friends for, if not to help each other solve problems?'

'That's very kindly put, Dimna,' the lion answered, 'but really there's nothing much the matter with me except a bad chill that makes my bones ache. I simply haven't felt like moving about much recently. No doubt it will soon pass away.'

Now it happened that while the lion was giving this false explanation, Schanzabeh was strolling about only half a mile away in the meadow directly below the king's window. They couldn't see him, but suddenly the bull bellowed two or three times, shattering the peaceful atmosphere with his mighty roar. The lion immediately began to shake and tremble.

'Your Majesty,' Dimna asked, 'whatever is the matter?'

'Oh, nothing, nothing. Just my chill acting up. Damn nuisance, really.'

'But, Sire, forgive me if I say I could hardly help noticing how you started to shiver when that strange grass-eater made his peculiar noise. Is it perhaps true that in some way this awful sound disturbs you?'

'Well, yes . . . I mean, no . . . that is to say . . . well, perhaps it does a bit. I mean it's so dreadfully loud, don't you think?'

'It certainly is, and most unpleasant too,' Dimna added. 'But surely that's no reason to let it bother us. It is only a noise, after all. And we really shouldn't let anything upset us until we know what it is, and whether or not it is a genuine threat to our well-being. Does Your Majesty remember the story about the fox and the drum? With permission, I'll remind you how it goes.'

The lion indicated his assent by nodding slightly.

The Fox and the Drum

'A certain fox entered a wood where a drum was hanging in a tree. When the wind blew, some of the branches knocked against the drum: "Boom . . . boom . . . rat-a-tat-tat!"

The fox froze in his tracks and listened. Then he crept towards the sound and saw this strange creature dangling near the ground from a branch. He decided that something of its size which made such a loud noise and lived in a tree must be good to eat. He suddenly rushed forward and leapt at the drum, tearing it down from the tree. Growling and biting, he ripped its skin off and broke it. But when he looked inside he found the drum was empty, and there was certainly nothing to eat.'

People who think that they have big brains more often only have big mouths.

Ornstein

54

'Hmmm,' said the lion, when Dimna had finished his story. 'Hmmm,' he said again, and rubbed his chin with a royal paw.

'Your Majesty,' Dimna said, 'what I am suggesting is that we investigate this grass-eater and find out what sort of beast he is. I am convinced that, like the drum, he makes a big noise but is really hollow and not worth worrying about. As you are feeling a bit unwell, may I volunteer to go out and meet this creature and find out something about him? It will only take a little time, and of course I'll return immediately to give you a complete report. Meanwhile, you can rest here in comfort.'

The lion drew back, raised his eyebrows, and pressed his lips together uncertainly. Then he smiled at Dimna and once again nodded his assent. Yet as soon as the jackal had thanked the king and left on his errand, the lion began to worry. In his mind all kinds of terrible fantasies began to brew.

I don't really know Dimna very well, he thought to himself. Perhaps it was a mistake to trust him so much. What if he now tells that creature how I tremble when it roars? Maybe he will decide that the grass-eater is stronger than I, and turn traitor. They will join forces and make plans to overthrow me, possibly even kill me. Dimna is so full of soothing words that he must have some hidden motive. Why did I allow him to go on his treacherous mission? Thus the lion leapt from one doubt into two or three more, and succeeded in working himself up into a state of great fear. He paced up and down in his chambers, fretting and chafing like a maniac. At last he looked out his window and saw

Dimna hurrying back up the trail towards the Tongue. By the time the jackal re-entered the Royal Lair the lion had regained his composure and looked as if nothing was bothering him.

Dimna informed the king that their mysterious grass-eater was only a bull. 'Although large and noisy,' Dimna said, 'he is in fact an extremely gentle creature.'

'But he must be very strong and therefore potentially dangerous,' the lion interjected.

'He may have strength, Your Majesty,' Dimna said, 'but I don't think he is a fighter. When I spoke to him, he gave the impression of someone who is both shy and kind. In fact, I found him such pleasant company that I was tempted to invite him back to meet Your Royal Highness. I think you would quite like him, Sire, and could reassure yourself that he certainly represents no threat to our security.'

'That sounds like an excellent idea,' the lion agreed. 'I think I would indeed enjoy meeting this bull, Dimna. Would you mind terribly going back to invite him to attend upon us at court?'

Dimna left immediately to find Schanzabeh, who was lying under a shady tree chewing his cud.

'Hello again, my friend,' Dimna said, and he lay down in the grass near Schanzabeh. The bull gave a nod and grunted his greetings, but continued chewing and chewing his cud.

'I have some news which may interest you,' the jackal said. 'As you know, I act as messenger for His Majesty, our king. I say "our king" quite deliberately because you, my friend, have now lived on His Majesty's territory for several weeks. And, I should add, you have enjoyed the pleasures of the kingdom without presenting yourself either to The King or to His Majesty's officers to obtain Official Grazing Permission.'

Schanzabeh paused briefly with his chewing, tilted his great head and looked curiously into the jackal's eyes.

'I have always maintained that this oversight on your part was unintentional,' Dimna continued, 'and that you meant no disrespect or harm to anyone. But there has been some talk at court to suggest that you are a willful trespasser and a dangerous interloper—a gate-crasher, so to speak, at our party. Such talk does you no good, my friend, for some have even hinted that The King should attack and kill you, or at least drive you away.'

Dimna bent his head to scratch at a flea behind his ear with a rear paw. When the itch was relieved he grinned up at Schanzabeh and continued.

'Fortunately, however, the lion is as just as he is strong; so far he has listened to my view that you have behaved this way out of ignorance, being a stranger and not knowing the customs of the place. I have assured him that had you known the land was His Majesty's, you certainly would have applied for OGP. His Majesty has now decided to settle this matter once and for

all, and this morning I am commanded to invite you to accompany me up the hill to the court. The King wishes to meet you and make up his own mind about your intentions.'

During this speech a growing apprehension arose in Schanzabeh's breast. He stopped chewing his cud, snorted uneasily, and stood up.

'Perhaps it would be wise for me to leave this area immediately.' he said. 'From what you say, it sounds as though I may be in some considerable danger.'

'No, no,' Dimna said, also rising, 'that is unnecessary. I am instructed by the lion to promise you safe passage to and from the court. Don't worry—no one will harm you. I think your wisest move would be to come with me and clear the matter up. It's merely a formality.'

'Nevertheless,' said the bull, 'I had no idea that things had come to such a pass. How can you promise me a safe journey?'

'Well, now,' said Dimna, thinking quickly, 'I promise you, by the ears of my brother jackal, Kalila, that you will have a safe journey. May they be bitten off if anything happens to you.'

'So be it,' declared Schanzabeh, and he sealed the bargain by lowering his great head and gently pressing noses with Dimna.

Dimna lost no time escorting Schanzabeh to court. But to the lion it seemed that a thousand years had passed. He was listening to some particularly tedious dispute of territory between several monkey families, trying desperately to keep his attention focused on banana tree boundaries and such nonsense. The rival factions squabbled back and forth in excited, high-pitched chatterings, shaking fists and hopping up and down. Suddenly the lion caught sight of Dimna loping up the path with the great bull following behind. The king was overcome with Schanzabeh's size and beauty. 'Now here is someone to have on your side,' he said to himself. 'What a creature!' Indeed the entire court was shocked into utter silence by the magnificence of the bull, and scrambled out of his way as he came closer to the Tongue.

Schanzabeh slowly approached the presence of the lion with lowered horns and knelt down before him. 'May it please Your Majesty, I beg forgiveness for my ignorant negligence in failing to salute Your Majesty before now,' he said, keeping his eyes on the ground. 'Had I realized I was in Your Majesty's territory, I would have presented myself sooner. But until recently I have always believed I was alone in this valley. Now that I am correctly informed, however, I am delighted with the opportunity of serving Your Majesty and the prospects of future companionship with the friendly creatures of Your Majesty's kingdom.'

These words of humility so ravished the king and his court that almost everyone immediately formed a good impression of the bull. A murmur of approval swept the crowd of onlookers.

'Stand up, stand up, good bull,' the lion roared, and everyone was quiet. 'Be welcome, and tell us what adventures have brought you to this place, and why it is that you are sometimes so noisy.'

'It is not so much adventures, Your Majesty, as miseries,' Schanzabeh said, as he rose to his full height.

Then, standing firm, in a voice filled with confidence and sincerity, Schanzabeh told his story of his loneliness in the valley. Everyone listened intently until he had finished.

'O bull, you sound a stalwart type, and I am impressed by your tale,' said the lion. 'You have no need to be lonely in my kingdom, and I invite you to remain here with us, sharing all that nature provides. I welcome you to our court, and feel so happy at your appearance in our midst that I hereby appoint you to the titles Prince of Bulls and Duke strange appoint of Beef!' A great ovation of roars, brayings, grunts, snorts, howls, yowls, hisses, whistles, and yells broke out from the rest of the animals, and the new Duke of Beef knelt down again at this sudden change in his fortune.

In due course the lion and the bull became great friends. The king consulted Schanzabeh on every matter, personal and political, and they rollicked about the countryside together mixing business and pleasure. It was obvious to everyone that the Duke of Beef was the lion's new favourite.

At first, Dimna tried to control his irritation at being displaced from the king's affections. But soon so much envy percolated into his breast that he could contain himself no longer, and he began muttering.

'How is it that I was so stupid as to serve The King and neglect my own interests? It was I who introduced the bull to the lion, but what rewards have I received? Do I have even one title, let alone two? Who enjoys the favours of The King which were previously mine? Oh, curses, curses, curses be on that wretched Prince of Bulls!' These mutterings by Dimna were a bit unfair, for Schanzabeh never failed to share any material benefits or privileges he received from the king with his original

benefactor, the jackal. 'I will always be in your debt,' he said one day to Dimna, 'for persuading me to appear before The King.' But it irked the jackal's pride that the bull received the lion's most intimate attention, while his own rewards mostly came—so to speak—second-hoof.

When he could not stand it any longer, Dimna went to Kalila and gave vent to his irritation. Kalila sat calmly on his haunches in front of his den as Dimna paced up and down before him, ranting and raving about the injustice of it all, and why had that damned Schanzabeh gained so many benefits while he was ignored? Eventually, Dimna's violent emotions spent themselves, and Kalila spoke.

'While I sympathize with your problem, brother, I'm afraid you have nobody to blame but yourself. You're upset now, but it was you that insisted on meddling in court affairs. What did you expect? Stick your paw in the fire, and you risk burning it. Your situation reminds me of the story of the dervish and the thief, and if you'll just sit down and calm yourself, I am going to tell it to you.' Kalila waited until Dimna had grumpily settled down beside him and then he spoke.

The Dervish and the Thief

'There was once a certain venerable dervish whose serious demeanour and reputation for devout behaviour so impressed those about him that he was eventually honoured by a visit from his king. This monarch experienced such a sublime sensation of spiritual uplift in the company of this "holy man" that, before his departure, he presented the dervish with a magnificent royal robe.

The dervish was affected by this gift in no small way. He soon took to wearing his new robe on every possible public occasion, and felt that this new mark of distinction entitled him, as it were, to strut about like a peacock which has suddenly realized the beauty of its plumage. His formerly shy and diffident manner in dealing with friends and acquaintances was gradually replaced by an authoritarian posture. He became bombastic and overbearing, opinionated and brusque; what little sense of humour he had ever possessed deserted him altogether. However, because the dervish's reputation as a man of wisdom appeared sanctified by the very presence of the royal robe, hardly anyone no-

ticed these changes in his character. People allowed
him to dominate social situations and were even
grateful to have such an indisputably "serious" man
bully them in this way. Almost everybody, that is, except for a certain thief who, for reasons of his own,
determined to steal the dervish's magnificent robe.

He appeared one morning at the dervish's home, requested a private interview, was admitted and, after
the necessary formalities, spoke as follows:

"O wise and illustrious sage, I come before you
empty-handed except for my determination to learn.
For several years your reputation as a good man has
inspired me towards spiritual improvement. Yet now I
sense that my only hope lies in being under your direct
guidance. Please consent, therefore, to take me as your
disciple that I might have at least some small chance of
finding the true path. However unworthy I may appear
today, I give my solemn promise that I shall endeavour
to serve you faithfully." It must be said in the dervish's
favour that this apparently submissive speech did not
at first attract him. His immediate inclination was to
sling the young man out on his ear. But he hesitated,
unsure in himself how to gauge the sincerity of the
thief's entreaty. After all, he *did* have something to
teach: he felt sure of that! And so far no one had ever
applied to become a bona fide disciple.

The thief instinctively guessed the dervish's inner
doubt, and realizing that he had nothing to lose,
quietly knelt down and hung his head—the perfect
picture of an abject supplicant. This act moved the
dervish to a decision. He placed his hands upon

the thief's shoulders and drew him back onto his feet.

"Arise, my son, arise," he said in a most solemn tone. "This is as much an auspicious occasion for me as it is for you. The time is indeed ripe for a disciple to sit, as it were, at my feet and partake of the small wisdom which Heaven has seen fit to vouchsafe me. Know, then, that I accept your application and feel sure that we can make effective efforts together."

It was not long before the thief came to live under the dervish's very roof. In all outward behaviour he appeared the model disciple, humbly serving the dervish in every particular and forcing himself to listen with rapt attention to all of the old man's most boring pontifications. One night, however, while the dervish was fast asleep, the thief stole the magnificent robe and everything else of value which he could carry away. The next morning the dervish was shattered to discover that all of his most prized possessions were missing. What had he done to deserve such a fate? What wrong attitude had he harboured to be betrayed in so thankless a manner?

Finding no answer to these questions, the dervish determined to track down his erstwhile disciple and ask him directly. Surely there must be some lesson in the fact that he had been so successfully duped by one who seemed so sincere; and, if he were lucky, he might even be able to recover his robe of honour. Thus it was that the dervish, taking only his begging bowl and his resolution, set out to learn what he could.

The thief's trail led away from the town, and by af-

ternoon the dervish found himself following a rough road through the mountains. He sat down on a rock to rest. Nearby he noticed two rams who were preparing to fight. They stood perhaps thirty paces apart, snorting and occasionally pawing the earth. Then, as if at a given signal, they charged, fiercely smashing their horns together with a loud crack which echoed from the surrounding peaks. The dervish watched this spectacle repeat itself over and over again until both the rams were dripping blood from their injuries. Still they went at it, relentlessly butting their heads together in a monotonous rhythm which became almost hypnotic: crack, echo, pause; crack, echo, pause.

From behind a rock a fox suddenly crept out. The dervish watched entranced as it nimbly stepped into the battle area and delicately began to lick up some of the rams' blood which had spattered on the stony ground.

So intent is the fox on relishing these free morsels that it fails to notice that the two rams, oblivious of any intruder, are realigning themselves so that he now stands directly in their next line of charge. Blinded with fury, the rams once again lower their horns and run full tilt towards each other. The fox raises his head only just in time to have his skull crushed between the smack of crashing horns. With barely an extra pause, the rams back off and resume their deadly butting; the fox lies dead but twitching, his brains strewn upon the ground.

Now this incident so shocks and horrifies the dervish that he immediately ups and hurries on his way, the echoes from the rams' ferocious battle serving, until he escapes earshot, to reinforce the dreadful image of the fox's sudden end. Evening approaches. The dervish pushes along at a good pace in order to reach the next town before nightfall. He barely manages to enter its gates before dark. Tired and still upset by the death of the fox, he seeks out lodging for the night. The first townsperson to offer him hospitality is an apparently kindly old woman who, as it happens, runs the local brothel. The dervish, knowing nothing of this, quietly goes off into a corner of the main room to say his prayers and meditate upon the day's events.

Among the madam's bevy of young girls whose favours she sells to the men of the town is an exceptionally pretty one who has formed a sincere and strong attachment with a true lover. This young woman and her gentleman guard themselves exclusively for each other, and moon about the brothel holding hands and casting one another fond glances like a lovesick cow and calf. Because this pretty courtesan will allow no man to approach her other than her lover, her turn- over decreases and the brothel suffers

loss of profits. This fact increasingly angers the madam, for her personal income, based on a half-share of what her girls earn from their men, begins to feel the pinch. And such is her greed that she is determined to end this nonsense once and for all that very night.

So while the dervish is sitting off in his corner, the brothel's business is proceeding as normal. Men arrive from time to time into the gentle candlelight of the main room and, under the madam's friendly management, pair off into various smaller, side bedrooms with the lady of their choice. The single exception, however, is this particular young woman and her lover, who are reclining on floor cushions off to one side drinking wine, laughing, whispering sweet nothings, and kissing as only true lovers can.

Pretending great delight in their happiness, the madam, all smiles and twinkling eyes, approaches the young lovers with a flask to refill their wineglasses. They hardly notice her appearance, simply hold out their glasses for more: it is easy for the old lady to slip a tiny opiate into the young man's drink. It is not long before he flops back upon the cushions and falls into a deep sleep. Greatly upset, his pretty young lady tries in vain to wake him, and fearful for his health, rushes out of the whorehouse to fetch a doctor.

Now that the young man lies alone upon the cushions, the madam creeps towards him through the dim light intent on deadly mischief. In her hand she carries a reed filled with a fine venomous powder. She reaches the young man, kneels down beside him and places one end of the reed in his mouth. She takes a deep breath and places the other end of the reed in her own, intending to blow the poison deep into his body. Unexpectedly, the young man burps. To the madam's horror, the full blast of his burp travels up through the reed and she feels all the poisonous powder being blown down her own throat. Clutching her neck, she reels back, staggers, and falls to the floor with loud groans of terror. Because the poison is extremely strong, she dies horribly in less than half an hour, and the doctor, who has arrived with the young courtesan, cannot even help to relieve the frenzy of her suffering. The poor dervish, trembling witness to all of this, sits astonished at the world's monstrous wickedness and thinks the night extremely long.

The next day he leaves the brothel and spends a fruitless day searching for his ex-disciple. Come evening, he again seeks out lodging in some house. This time he is taken in by a friendly cobbler who says, "You are most welcome to stay in my house, friend, but unfortunately tonight I must go out to a business party which I cannot avoid. My wife will look after you and see that you are comfortable. She'll prepare you a meal and you can sleep on that workbench over there in the corner. If you lay out some of my skins in a pile, you'll find they make quite a tolerable mattress. Now, if you'll excuse me, I'm off, and we'll see each other in the morning. Good night."

The dervish thanks the cobbler for his kindness and after enjoying a simple but delicious meal prepared by his wife, settles down on the workbench to say his prayers and go to sleep.

Now the cobbler's wife is young and pretty, and has a sometime lover who is handsome and witty. This loving couple meets from time to time at this place or that, thanks to the help of the next-door neighbour's wife, an old bag who delights in playing the go-between to their naughtiness. When the dervish is asleep, the young wife goes to the neighbour and whispers in her ear, "My old man's out on the town tonight and will no doubt come home late and drunk. So, if you can, please go and tell you-know-who that the coast is clear for a bit of fun and that I'd love to see him if he's free."

The old bag grabs her shawl, and cackling and rubbing her hands together in delight, rushes out of her house to deliver the message to the young swain. But as chance would have it, the cobbler's party ends early, and tipsy with drink, he arrives home at exactly the same time as his wife's lover is approaching his front door. The old cobbler, no fool, and having already heard a vague rumour that his wife is enjoying a bit on the side, immediately comprehends what is going on. With a brief glower at the young man, who by this time is pretending to gaze intently at the stars, whistling softly to himself as if he hadn't a care in the world, the cobbler rushes into his house in a rage.

Yanking his young wife out of bed by her beautiful black hair, he throws her over his knee and begins to beat the living daylights out of her. She screams and yells for him to stop, but to no avail, and the cobbler continues until his arm is tired and his wife's bottom, if you could see it, all black and blue. He hauls her over to one side of the room and ties her naked body firmly to one of the rough-hewn roof pillars with some handy leather thongs. Puffing with rage and exertion, he jerks her head back and spits out his first words since entering the house:

"I'll teach you to cuckold me, you little hussy! You can damn well spend the night standing up here, because I'm not having you in bed with me." So saying, he tears off his clothes and throws himself into bed, angry at her and angry at himself for being angry, an avalanche of self-pity forcing him to cry hot, sticky tears onto the pillow until he falls asleep and begins to snore.

Now as you may well imagine, it is impossible for the old dervish to sleep through this melodrama. Covered by his cloak and lying still as a mouse, his heart pounding furiously with unexpected excitement, he can't help witnessing this scene of domestic violence by the dim moonlight which barely illumines the room from two low windows. And although now the old cobbler is snoring and dreaming away (I would guess of rams, stags, oxen, and other beasts with horns grafted to their foreheads), in no way can the poor dervish get back to sleep. Soon he hears a scratching and a creaking from the back door and then sees the wheedling old biddy neighbour sneaking softly into the room on tiptoe, pausing to look about, and approaching the young wife tied to the pillar.

"Dear, oh, dear, oh, deary me," the old crone whispers softly. "What have we here? I heard a dreadful commotion and thought you might be dead!"

The young wife responds with a sigh. "Well, you're not far wrong," she whispers. "Some malicious tattle-

tale or other has been busy spreading stories about me,
and this brought the old man home early in a fury. He
spanked me so hard I thought I would die and as if that
wasn't enough, he tied me up to this post! Oh, how my
bottom aches and throbs!'' The young wife pauses for a
moment to let her neighbour savour this tidbit, and
then proceeds as follows:

"If you would be a true friend and a charitable
neighbour, I beg you to untie me and put yourself in my
place for only a few hours. I really must go and see
you-know-who and tell him what's happened. Please,
please, don't say no, I can't bear to be apart from him
any longer. I'll come back as soon as I can—I promise."

Moved with compassion and being a hearty well-
wisher to the sweets of adultery, the old bag readily
agrees. Very quietly, the two women change places,
and the young wife, throwing on a few clothes, sneaks
out of the house to snatch a few tender hours in the
arms of her lover. The dervish, who has heard and seen
all this deviousness, moodily decides that he can no
longer accuse the cobbler of cruelty.

He is just on the point of drifting back to sleep when
the cobbler wakes up and, feeling the potential onset of
contrition, softly calls out his wife's name in the dark.
The terrified old biddy dares not answer, for she knows
her voice will give the game away. Again the cobbler
calls, and still there is no answer. He tries a third time.
Silence. Furious beyond endurance, the cobbler leaps
out of bed and yells, "God's Teeth, woman—will you
not answer me?" He picks up a knife and flies upon
her, at one slash cutting off, so he thinks, his wife's

nose. Holding out the bloody proboscis in his hand, he says, "Here you are, tramp! Take this as a little present to your wagtail in a corner."

The poor old neighbour lady, though in the utmost agony, dares not so much as whimper. The cobbler drops the nose at her feet and stumbles back to bed. The dervish lies rigid on the workbench trying not to vomit.

By and by, when everything is again quiet except for the cobbler's renewed snoring, the young wife returns from her sweet pleasures and, as you may well imagine, is horrified beyond measure to find her faithful friend missing a nose. Begging a thousand hearty pardons, she unbinds the old crone and ties herself in place. The wretched biddy returns home carrying her nose in her hand.

Some hours later the young wife begins to moan pitifully to herself, and, when she is sure her husband is awake and listening, prays loudly as follows:

"O Most Powerful Deity, who knowest the secrets of all hearts, behold an innocent abused without cause. Thou knowest my chastity, yet my husband has done me open wrong by most cruelly defacing me. If what I say is true, I pray Thee, O God, to undo his barbarity and restore to me my nose."

At these words the cobbler sits bolt upright in bed and cries, "Evil bitch, what wicked prayer is this? Don't you realise that the pleadings of a whore defile the ears of God? True prayer must issue from a clean heart, and yours is like a filthy sink!"

But the wife ignores his reprimand and cries out in seeming exultation, "Hallelujah—thanks be to God!

Hallelujah—Thou hast done it, O Almighty One! A miracle! A miracle!'' She bursts into a flood of thankful tears, so powerful is her feigned emotion. The sceptical cobbler quickly lights a candle and rushes to his wife. He finds her nose perfect, no mark upon her face, and is thunderstruck, falls to his knees, kisses her feet, and begs forgiveness. He unties her, leads her back to bed, and by a thousand caresses strives to make her forget his earlier brutality.

Meanwhile, the noseless crone returns home wondering to herself how to explain her loss to her husband, the barber. She sits besmeared in blood on her edge of their bed until dawn when the barber wakes up. He stretches out his arms in the dark, yawns, and coughs. ''Another day begins, dear wife, another day,'' he says sleepily. ''Please be so good as to fetch me my comb case and razors. I have an important customer to shave at first light this morning.''

The old bag pulls her shawl tightly around her face and shuffles off to do his bidding while the barber lights his bedside candle and begins to dress. She takes her time, and returns bringing only the comb case.

''But where are the razors, woman?'' he demands. ''Are you deaf? Fetch the razors!''

Off she goes again, very slowly and silently. The barber, dressing hurriedly, reaches out his hand absentmindedly when she returns. But the clever crone passes him the razors blade forward and not in their hafts, so that one nicks the flesh of his finger.

''Stupid cow!'' the barber yells, and hurls the razors back at her so that they scatter about the room.

"Aiee, aiee!" screams the biddy as loud as she can. "My nose! My nose!" She doubles over in seeming agony and quickly picks up one of the razors and smears it with some of her blood. "Aiee, aiee!" she screams. "Murder! Murder!"

The dumbfounded barber cannot believe his ears, and runs over with the candle. Straightaway she shows him the blood, her severed nose, the razor, and continues to scream the house down. Kinfolk and friends rush into the room, seize the seemingly vicious barber and try to comfort the hysterical old woman.

Later in the morning the barber is escorted to the sessions court and accused of his cruel crime. Convinced of his guilt, he offers no defense and stands unhappily hanging his head for shame.

"For your terrible deed," intones the judge when he has heard the case, "I sentence you to the punishment of having your own nose slashed off with a razor! This crime is one of the most bestial and dreadful ever brought before my court, and there is no other way I can find to dispense justice."

But before the hapless barber can be led away, the dervish, who has followed the crowd into the courtroom, leaps up, throws his arms wide apart, and cries:

"Hold, O Judge! Hold! You do not know the full story! Let me speak, for I cannot bear it any longer!"

"What is the meaning of this outburst?" snaps the judge. "Explain yourself, friend, and you had better make it good or I shall clap you behind bars for demeaning the dignity of this courtroom with such irregular behaviour."

"Your Honour, in order to seek out justice in this case we must return to the beginning and hear how my only disciple stole the magnificent robe presented to me by The King. Strange as it seems, everything is connected, and I beg permission to tell the whole story so that we may all understand what has really happened."

Mention of the king magnetized the judge's attention. Fearing that the dervish, whatever his appearance, might be someone of importance, he allowed him to go on. The dervish, omitting no detail, told his own story from the moment he was given the royal robe. Everyone in the courtroom—bailiffs, onlookers, idlers, supplicants, plaintiff, lawyers, clerks, and general hangers-on—listened entranced, and at the end the dervish concluded as follows:

"Your Honour, had I not accepted the robe from ambition, the thief would never have robbed me. Had the fox not licked up the battle blood from greediness, the rams would not have killed him. Had the madam not tampered with the course of true love, she would never have been poisoned. Had the barber's wife not meddled in the adultery of the cobbler's wife, she would never have lost her nose. And from all this story one short lesson can be learned: those who indulge in greed (whatever its disguise) cannot hope for the influence of good."

Such was the impact of the dervish's story that the judge adjourned the court for the rest of the day in celebration of receiving this wisdom. And everyone went home and lived out their lives as best they could.'

'I follow the drift of your story, brother,' Dimna said to Kalila, 'and agree that I wouldn't be in my present predicament had I minded my own business. Given the choice, I certainly wouldn't behave in the same way again. But I'm in it up to my neck now, so what can I do? I feel so spiteful towards Schanzabeh that I could burst.'

Dimna nipped repeatedly at a flea on his left shoulder, snarling softly as his teeth tugged through the fur. Satisfied, he stood up, shook himself, and began to pace about. 'One way or another,' he grumbled, 'I must devise a plan to slander and discredit the bull in The King's eyes in order to regain my former position. Like everyone, the Duke of Beef must have some misdemeanour in his past which he would prefer to keep hidden. By hook or by crook I'll find out some secret about him and tell it to the lion. After all, it probably is in the best interest of the community that The King recognize the real nature of this sneaky grass-eater.'

'Come, come,' Kalila quickly said. 'Do you mean to say you seriously think there is danger in The King's friendship with the Duke? You're letting your jealousy run away with you, and looking for some feeble justification for your actions, however implausible.'

Dimna stopped short in his tracks and his hackles rose as he faced his brother with a threatening stare.

'Now look, you,' he growled. 'That's enough of your rotten, amateur analysis of my motives. It's a very well known fact that favouritism at court leads to potentially rebellious rivalries. Those who are left out of The

King's favours always harbour grudges against those
who are rewarded with his attention.'

'Okay, okay,' Kalila laughed, backing away a step or
two. 'But how on earth are you going to succeed in
undermining Schanzabeh's reputation? At present he
seems pretty well entrenched in The King's affections.
Not to mention the obvious fact that he is considerably
bigger and stronger than you.'

'You speak like a fool,' Dimna retorted, 'if you assume that only the big and strong can seek revenge.
More often than not, it is the poor thief who robs the
rich and distinguished victim, the insignificant germ
that destroys the great and mighty, the coward that
kills the hero. Since I have had to endure your tedious
stories on more than one occasion, I'll thank you now
to hear mine about the crow, the snake, and the jackal,
which illustrates this very point.'

*Our
doctrine
is not
a dogma,
but a guide
to action.*

Marx
and
Engels

The Crow, the Snake, and the Jackal

'There was a crow who built her nest in the top of a great old tree. Once she had laid her eggs, behold, a snake slithered from a hole at the rotten root of the old tree and, zigzag, climbed to the top and sucked them dry. In great distress the crow flew to her friend the jackal to seek advice.

"I'm going to get that bastard whatever it costs," she said.

"How do you plan to do it?" asked the jackal quietly.

"As soon as I catch him asleep," answered the crow, "I'm going to land on his head and peck out his eyes. That snake will never find his way to another nest once I've finished with him."

"I see," said the jackal, licking his upper lip. "I don't like the odds," he continued softly, shaking his head. "No, I don't like them one little bit. If I were you, friend, I would find another method of revenge, one which involves less risk to yourself. Otherwise the same thing might happen to you which happened to the crane that tried to kill a crab. Do you remember the story?"

The Crane and the Crab

crane once dwelt upon a pleasant lake placed among little hills spread over with herbs and flowers. He lived upon such fish as he could catch, and for many years got plenty. But at length, becoming old and feeble and unable to plunge into the water with his former speed, the crane was driven to fly in the air and feed only on the occasional cricket. Soon he was almost starving.

While the crane was poised in the bankside shallows one morning, sighing and looking mighty melancholy, there wandered sideways by a huge old freshwater crab who asked him what the trouble was.

'Oh,' replied the crane, 'I'm depressed by the conversation I overheard between two fishermen yesterday. That's all.'

'And what did they say?' asked the crab.

'Do you really want to know?' answered the crane. 'It's not very pleasant news, and I have no wish to burden you.'

'Don't worry,' the crab said. 'Tell me about it. I'm interested.'

'Well, I was standing around one-leggedly over in that patch of reeds at the other end of the lake. The sun was shining fiercely, and I must have dozed off. Anyway, I didn't hear these two men approach. Their voices woke me but they were too close for me to move without risk. I stood stockstill, camouflaged by the reeds, and listened. "If we dug a trench through the left bank, we could drain this lake and catch all the fish in it," said one. "True," said his friend, "and there are many fish here. But I think I have a better idea. You know that smaller lake higher up in the hills, a mile or so away? Well, it also teems with fish and would be even easier to drain. Let's do that smaller one first, and later, on another day, we can come back here."

'I'm sure they mean business,' continued the crane, 'and when they return, that means the end of the fish and therefore the end of me. Without fish to feed on, my days are numbered. I am too old to fly about in search of a new home and start all over again. I am waiting for the day the fishermen come back, and facing the inevitability of death. There is nothing to be done except to wait, and learn to accept my fate.'

'Very interesting,' said the crab, and she slid off into the lake to seek out the President of the Fishes. He was taking a nap—floating almost motionless near the lake bottom among some waving weeds—a huge old carp that had seen at least a dozen summers and weighed nearly six pounds.

'Mr. President,' said the crab, 'Mr. President—please wake up!'

'Burble,' said President Fish, and in a start his body

swished left and right until he saw who it was. 'What is it, Madam Crab,' he said irritably. 'Why have you interrupted my siesta?'

'President Fish,' answered the crab, 'it's about the fishermen coming to drain the lake. It's an emergency, and I think you had better call your cabinet together for a special meeting.'

This is exactly what happened once the crab had told him the full story. After the meeting the president's most intimate advisers fanned out into every nook and cranny of the lake to declare an Extraordinary Session of the Parliament of Fishes. Soon a great hubbubble arose from the traditional meeting spot deep in the middle of the lake. When all the fishy debates were done, and every opinion heard, a vote was taken which carried the motion to speak to the crane. That afternoon the fish swam towards the old bird in a great wedge-shaped armada with their president in the vanguard.

'Although you are our enemy,' he said from a safe distance, 'we feel we must have a word with you about our common danger.'

'But of course, by all means,' responded the crane in a somewhat lacklustre tone. 'What can I do for you?'

'First, please simply answer this question. Are you quite positive that you heard two men saying they intended to drain the entire lake?'

'Yes, I heard it with my own ears. I swear it by all the feathers on my body.'

'Well, then,' said President Fish, 'we are both in the same dilemma. For if we who are your food die, you die too, old bird.'

'I am well aware of the delicate ecological balance which is involved,' the crane remarked testily. 'In fact I have personally resigned myself to my own death, and sincerely feel the inescapable doom which awaits—'

'But is there nothing we can do to protect ourselves?' interrupted President Fish.

'No, I think not,' said the crane. 'We do not between us have sufficient power to withstand two determined men. There is only one way out, but I doubt you will try it, for it involves placing your complete trust in me.'

'For love of the lake, tell us anyway!' President Fish exclaimed. 'What have we to lose even if it fails? Say on, for we have not the least idea of what to do, and have come to hear your advice.'

The crane slowly rotated his head on the end of his long neck and carefully tucked his left leg up under his wing. 'There is a rather special pond not far from here,' he said at length, his little jet eyes peering past the tip of his beak. 'The water is cool and clear, and the bottom so deep that men could never drain it. More important, it is uninhabited by fish. My idea would be to fly you there, one or two at a time, depending on size. You could grip the feathers on my back with your mouths, and strength permitting, I estimate I could make four or five trips per day.'

'But how do we know this is not a trick?' asked President Fish.

'There,' said the crane, 'I predicted you wouldn't trust me. So, what is to be done except wait around for the fishermen? It won't be long now; they should finish with the smaller lake inside a couple of months.'

'Would you take me upon your back to see this pond?' asked President Fish. 'I could swim about in it and verify the truth of what you say, and then you could bring me back here to tell the others. Will you also guarantee a complete truce between us during this difficult period of transition? No fish-eating until we are newly settled and things return to normal?'

'Why, of course I will,' answered the crane. 'Certainly, certainly. Maybe you would care to have a trial run now?'

'Why not?' President Fish answered. 'There's still plenty of daylight left.'

It was agreed. The crane dove underwater so President Fish could obtain a good grip on the shoulder feathers with his mouth. He surfaced with the big fish nestled on his back. When all was balanced, the crane flew slowly off, mustering every bit of his remaining strength, and shortly arrived at the pond. President Fish plopped off the crane's back and spent a good quarter of an hour exploring the locale.

'The pond is everything the crane says it is,' President Fish told all the other fish excitedly when he had returned. 'I urge you, therefore, to accept his offer. Let the great exodus begin! It is our only hope of survival. Three cheers for the crane. Hip hip . . .'

'Hooray!' sang out all the gathered congregation of fishes. 'Hip hip, hooray!' Even the old she-crab joined in the cheering and waved her claws about in the air.

The next day the crane made five trips carrying away a total of seven fish, four little ones in pairs and three large ones riding solo. But he flew his finny passengers to a rocky hilltop out of sight of the lake, and—when they could no longer hold their breaths and released their holds from his feathers—he flung them violently off his back so they lay gasping for water in the sunlight. Then he killed them and devoured them. Thus for many days he continued filling his belly, and soon grew sleek and glossy-feathered.

However, one morning the she-crab requested a ride to the pond, as she missed a particular tench friend who had flown on before her. The crane, realizing that the crab was a potential troublemaker, readily agreed—determined to drop her from the air on to the rocks below and smash her to pieces. The crab scrambled up on to the crane's back and tightly clasped his feathers with her legs and claws. They mounted into the skies and soon left the lake far behind, but after many minutes the crab still could not see the famous pond.

'Friend, friend,' she cried out over the wind which rushed past her, 'how much farther to the cool, clear water which we have heard so much about?'

'Ha ha!' the crane yelled back over his shoulder. 'You dumb crustaceous bitch—there is no pond for you! Look yonder to those rocks and you'll see the garbage heap where I am dumping you!' Sure enough, the crab could see in the distance great piles of fish heads and fishbones which the crane had scattered about on the hilltop. He now began to swoop sharply left and right, trying to shake the crab off his back. But an instant later he felt first one then the other of the crab's powerful claws grip his neck as tightly as a blacksmith's pincers. The claws squeezed so hard that the old crane began to gasp and tears ran from his eyes. Madam Crab carefully pulled herself forward and shouted down his earhole:

'If I were you, foul fowl, I'd stop this nonsense and make a nice soft landing immediately. Otherwise I shall cut off your head as clean as a man lops through a lotus stalk with his hunting knife, and we shall perish together.'

'Hrvvck aahh krrr,' the crane rasped out from deep in his throat. 'Stop, stop, you're strangling me! I can't see! Stop, for God's sake, so I can land!'

Madam Crab relaxed her grip perhaps a millimeter: the old crane glided ever so gently to the ground.

'Sit down, you evil trickster, so I can climb off your back,' the crab ordered.

'I was only joking,' the crane said in great pain, folding his legs and lowering his body to the earth.

'Tell me another,' said the crab, and with a mighty squeeze she shut her claws and cut his head off clean as a whistle. When she had recovered and wept over the bones of her friends, the crab made her way back to the lake and told all the remaining fish of her adventure with the treacherous crane. Needless to say, they gave her many thanks for their deliverance, but poor President Fish somehow became the scapegoat for their collective poor judgment, and was hounded from office and never forgiven.''

*Fine
feathers
do not make
fine birds.*

Saying

"Caw!" said the crow, when her jackal friend had stopped speaking. "That's a bit of your old blood and thunder. Whew! I'd sure like to do to the snake what that crab did to the crane, but I see what you mean about my plan being risky. Caw! That was a nice story, though. Thanks!"

"Yes, but it's only an analogy," said the jackal. "Your situation is a bit different. The crab was lucky, you see; but you mustn't trust to luck in your own revenge."

"What do you think I should do, then?" asked the crow. "Have you got an idea?"

"Well, yes—as a matter of fact, I have. It'll take a bit of courage to execute, but I think you're up to it. If you like, come a bit closer and I'll whisper it to you."

And so the crow hopped over next to where the jackal sat and listened while he quietly outlined his plan. Every now and again she jumped up into the air from excitement and shouted "Caw!" or "That's terrific!" and the jackal paused to smile at her pleasure.

Later that day the crow flew slowly over the nearest village until she spotted a woman of rank who was taking her bath on top of a house, having laid her clothes and trinkets aside. The crow darted suddenly down and snatched up a valuable necklace; the woman cried out, raised a great hullabaloo among all the people in the village. The crow hovered about with the necklace dangling from her beak until a crowd gathered and threw up sticks and stones hoping to make her drop it. Then she led them all a merry chase across the fields, flying low and keeping just ahead.

Once or twice she landed and hopped about out of reach, shaking her head violently from side to side so that the necklace flashed in the sunlight and the crowd worked itself into a rage to get its hands upon her.

At last the crow came to her old tree and dropped the necklace down the snake's hole. The villagers ran up and began digging among the roots while cursing and yelling at that damned crow perched in the tree above. Soon the snake slithered out among them. The mob bashed his head until he lay twitching dead. Then they recovered the necklace. Thus with one simple revenge the crow quitted the many injuries done her by the egg-sucking snake.'

"But strangest of all, the most incomprehensible thing, is that there are authors who can choose such subjects to write about. This, I confess, is completely inexplicable, it's like . . . no, no, I can't understand it at all.

Gogol

Dimna paused for a few moments at the end of this tale. 'You see, brother, physical strength alone does not always count in the success of an enterprise. Wit, skill, and strategy can also be key factors. The improbable can be brought to pass with willpower and determination.'

'In theory I certainly agree with you,' Kalila observed. 'But Schanzabeh is no lazy fool. He's not only big and strong, but he's smart too! One could even describe him as subtle and wise. He's no creature of impulse, but habitually seeks the advice of others before deciding what to do and—'

'You're right there,' Dimna interrupted, and a sly grin quickly spread across his muzzle. 'And to whom does the Duke always come running for personal advice? Me! And why? Because it was I who originally introduced His Grace at court with a guarantee of safety. He trusts me and believes anything I say. Furthermore, he has not the slightest hint that I've begun to loathe the very sight of him. No, Kalila. You're imagining this Prince of Bulls to be something absolutely fantastic and myself but a pathetic little idiot. Pathetic and little as I am, however, I'll play him a trick he won't soon forget. Remember what the hare did to the lion in the story of the same name?'

The Lion and the Hare

'Various animals once lived in a delightful forest surrounded by many pleasant meadows. Bloody kills by a fierce and hungry lion, however, continually shattered the peace.

Finally the surviving beasts held a meeting to discuss how they might organize themselves. They sent a delegation which cautiously approached the lion one morning with a compromise.

"O Lion," said the spokesbeast, an elderly and distinguished gazelle, "your appetite for flesh makes chaos of our lives. We tremble to think of your powerful jaws tearing at our throats. Such a perpetual state of anxiety is no way to live, and therefore we would like to propose the alternative concept of regulated sacrifice. Each of our families will offer up one of its members and daily we shall select by lottery one of them to become your food. Not only will this method save you much time in stalking and catching your prey, but also it will reintroduce some semblance of order into our lives. Some will be up for the chop, of course, but at least the rest of us can continue our lives in relative tranquillity. In short, we will contract to feed you every day from our own flesh and blood."

"I don't object to the idea," said the lion, "but how do I know I can trust you to deliver?"

"A good question, Your Powerfulness, a good question," replied the gazelle. "But you don't need to trust us at this stage. All you need to do is allow us time for a test: if we don't deliver as we promise, you can resume your former ways and kill us at random. You really have nothing to lose, O Mighty One."

"Hmm," said the lion. "All right, we'll try this regulated sacrifice plan of yours from this afternoon. Deliver me someone to eat by four o'clock. If it works, so much the better; but if it fails, be warned that I shall descend among you with terrible anger and kill at twice the rate of anything you've experienced so far."

Thus it was that for many weeks the lion thrived under what became known as the RSP lottery. Of course the other animals were saddened by the personal loss of any individual family member who was sacrificed; but they felt there was nothing they could do to improve the situation.

One day a certain hare won the lottery. It was by now customary for the sacrificial winner to spend a period of quiet and meditation in order to compose his or her mind before being escorted to the lion. After saying his goodbyes to various weeping relatives and good friends, the hare sat apart for an hour or so. Then he addressed a few of the official lottery administrators as follows:

"I have a small final request to make of you which

will in no way endanger anyone else. Please delay my escort to the lion by an hour or more in order that he will get hungry and wonder whether or not his food is coming. Then allow me to approach him alone, for I have a plan which may free us once and for all from the tyranny of this bully."

"Since you are to die in any case," said a huge old boar, after conferring with his fellow administrators, "we see no reason to disallow your request. I cannot, however, conceal from you that we are highly amused that a mere big-ears-and-cottontail presumes to believe himself a match for old Death Jaws himself. Still, any chance is better than none—so good luck to you, my son!"

The hare tarried along the way until he was very late indeed. When at last he reached the lion's den, he called out in a meek and hesitant voice, "Oh, Mr. Lion . . . Mr. Lion. . . . Where are you, Sir?"

"I'm right here, you dolt," the lion answered as he rushed out from behind a nearby tree. "Who the hell are you and what is the meaning of this intolerable delay? Where is my food?"

"It's been stolen, Sir, by another lion. I tried to stop him, but—"

"What?" roared the lion. "Stolen by another lion?"

"Yes, Sir. I was escorting my cousin to you for the four o'clock appointment when suddenly a rather unprepossessing member of your species attacked us and snatched up my cousin.

" 'Stop, stop,' I cried out. 'You can't do that. You're taking the food of the lion who owns this territory.'

" 'Hah,' he answered back in a most arrogant way. 'And who's going to stop me, you little flop-eared pip-squeak?'

" 'I'll have to report you to the lion who is expecting the food you've just stolen,' I said. 'I doubt he'll be exactly pleased with your poaching.'

" 'Oh, yes, your mighty master,' he says. 'I've heard of him. Sits about all day and waits for his food to be delivered to him. Some kind of rough, tough lion that is! You just tell him for me that the prey belongs to the hunter. If he wants this tidbit back, he can come and claim it from me if he dares. Hah! Meanwhile, tell him I shall take whatever I want whenever I want it from this area. He can have the leftovers if there are any, and consider himself lucky.' With that he ran off into the forest with my cousin in his jaws."

"Where is he?" spat the lion, rigid with rage, muscles quivering along his great back. "Where is this foul-mouthed interloper who steals my food?"

"I did follow him, Sir. I know his hiding place. But I think it might be dangerous to approach him just now."

"What?" the lion roared. "Dangerous, you say? Why, I'll teach this mangy amateur a lesson he won't forget. Dangerous? Grrrrr! Listen, you stupid twitch-nose: take me to him now! Or I'll break your back so fast you won't know what hit you. Now get moving!"

"Yes, Sir," said the hare in simulated terror. "If you insist, Sir."

"I *do!*" roared the lion so loudly the hare was momentarily knocked off his feet.

The hare quickly scampered off into the forest. By

and by he led the lion to a deep pit which he knew was partly filled with water. He paused near some bushes and clumps of grass which obscured its edge and whispered to the lion, "Please, Sir, I'm afraid to go any closer alone. The other lion is hiding down a hole just ahead. Let me stay right next to you and I shall point him out."

The lion nodded his assent and the two of them very quietly crept up to the pit's edge together. They were

just coming through the greenery when the hare said urgently, "There, Sir! There he is, and that's my cousin!"

The lion stood up suddenly and gave a thunderous battle roar. Its echo shot back at him from the other side of the pit. The hare instantly scuttled in between the lion's forelegs, and when the lion looked down into the pit, sure enough he saw another lion standing over a hare— his hare!

With all his strength he leapt to the attack. The hare flattened himself to the ground and the lion sailed over him to land with a terrific splash in the pit below.

It did not take the lion long to drown. Every time he loudly cursed the hare for his treachery, more water rushed down his throat. Soon he was spluttering and choking his life away. After a while the hare hopped home to tell all the other animals the good news.'

*The
poor beetle
that we
tread upon
In corporal
sufferance
feels as great
a pang
As when
a giant dies.*

Shakespeare

'Do you really think you can get away with something like that?' Kalila asked as soon as Dimna had stopped. 'What if your deceit results in Schanzabeh's death? Surely to harm by dishonest means someone so obviously good is a great sin! Do you doubt that God will see and know your real character? Oh, Dimna, you deceive yourself!'

'Say what you like,' Dimna retorted, 'but my mind is made up. Even if it costs me my life, I aim to discredit Schanzabeh in The King's eyes. Speak not to me of honesty or dishonesty, for they're not worth a fig in this life. Come what may, I am determined to test my wit and vent my hatred to the very last breath.'

So saying, Dimna left Kalila and disappeared into the forest where he remained in hiding for several days rehearsing his plans. When he eventually reappeared, it was from the shaded edge of a glossy green meadow one morning when the lion just happened to be passing. The king was alone and about his business, striding briskly down the main path in a very regal manner, head held high and his mane billowing out behind him.

'Ho, Dimna, Dimna!' he called out, when he caught sight of the jackal in the distance. 'Dimna, come here!'

Looking very pensive and dejected, Dimna shambled through the long grass into the sunlight towards the king. As he moved, his head hung low and his tail was tucked up between his rear legs. Perceiving that Dimna appeared to be in a bad way, the lion left the path and strode through the grass to meet him.

'What's up, Dimna?' the lion asked as he approached. 'You look like death dipped in misery. No one has seen you for days. Are you ill?'

Slowly, the jackal raised his head to look into the king's large amber eyes. 'No, Your Majesty, I'm not ill,' he answered in a soft voice. He paused for a moment, blinked in the sunlight. 'But I am worried, Your Majesty,' he sighed, shaking his head from side to side, 'very worried indeed.'

'Good heavens!' the lion expostulated. 'Whatever can it be that has so upset you? Come, Dimna—sit yourself down here with me and relax. We're alone and can talk in private. What's the matter? Tell me all about it.' The lion swished his tail around the left of his rump before settling down into the soft grass.

'Thank you, Your Majesty,' Dimna said, as he too sat down. 'You're very kind to me. But I don't know how to begin, so terrible is the news I bring.'

'What's that you say?' the lion interrupted, and an edge of brusqueness crept into his voice. 'What's terrible? What news? What are you talking about, Dimna?'

'Your Majesty,' Dimna replied, nearly whispering, 'three days ago someone whose integrity and judgement I value most highly told me some very distressing news. Since then I've been debating with myself whether I should pass the information on to Your Highness or not. It worries me to be the bearer of bad news, and I only hope you will remember my faithful service to you in the past.'

'Don't worry, Dimna,' the lion reassured the jackal, 'you can be quite open with me. You know full well that I hold you in the highest regard, and will listen to anything you might say.'

'Thank you, Your Majesty,' the jackal replied. 'Your confidence in my poor abilities gives me enough courage to proceed. But I must warn Your Majesty that you will find what I have to say unbelievable and incredible. When I first heard the story, my initial reaction was to discount it as sheer rumour and gossip. It sounded so improbable that I immediately tried to forget it. But I couldn't, and the more I thought about it, the more I came around to the opinion that perhaps you should be alerted, just in case it was true.'

The lion stood up impatiently and began to pace back and forth in the long grass. 'But what is it, Dimna?' he asked. 'What have you heard?'

Dimna stood up respectfully before his king.

'No, no. You sit down and take it easy,' the lion said, waving a paw in the general direction of the ground. 'Just sit down and give me a full report. Never mind my moving about; I'm listening.' The jackal settled back on his haunches and the lion resumed his pacing.

'Well, Your Majesty, put it this way,' Dimna began. 'The more I thought about it, the more I realized you would have to be told. The matter concerns not only the stability of the realm, but possibly even your personal safety as well. Frankly, I dreaded being the one to tell you, and half hoped you would have heard about it from someone else. But I am past caring about myself now. Whatever the consequences, I would be guilty of a dereliction in my duty or, even worse, a potential accomplice to treason if I didn't tell you what I know.'

'Absolutely right,' the lion said, and he stopped in front of Dimna and looked him straight in the eyes. 'If it's a matter of internal security, you should tell me right away. Now for heaven's sake, jackal—stop pussyfooting around and get on with it. Spit it out!'

'Well, Your Majesty, what I have heard concerns Schanzabeh. I am very reliably informed that the Duke has been meeting in secret with certain other animals in the kingdom with the idea of leading a rebellion to overthrow you. I am sorry to say it, but Schanzabeh wants to be king himself!'

The lion's eyes widened and his body stiffened into stillness. 'That's impossible!' And he began pacing back and forth, more vigorously this time, muttering to himself in a low growl.

The sun had risen higher in the cloudless sky. Along the northern edge of the meadow the many greens of the forest shimmered in the late morning heat. As he repeated his route over and over again in front of the jackal, the lion wore down a path in the grass. Dimna sat perfectly still, expressionless, facing south towards the river with a blank stare.

'Who told you this?' asked the lion as he paced. 'Who gave you this information, Dimna?'

'A friend of mine, Your Majesty, of the highest integrity. A creature whom I have never known to tell an untruth.'

'Yes, yes,' the lion said, 'but who?'

'Your Majesty, with all due respect,' Dimna began cautiously, 'I have promised on my oath never to identify my source. I cannot tell you who it is without a betrayal of his confidence in me. I beg you not to press me on the matter. My friend is afraid that he will be implicated in the affair, no matter how innocent he is of any conspiracy. He is genuinely afraid, Your Majesty, but I know him to be honest and free of any involvement. He accidentally overheard this story when some relative of his was approached to attend one of these secret meetings. However, I dare not tell you his name.'

'Hmm,' the lion said to himself as he moved over the trampled grass. He strode back and forth a while longer and then came and squatted beside Dimna.

'The story's unsubstantiated, then, eh?' he said. 'I don't believe it anyway. It's absurd. You mean to say Schanzabeh, the gentle grass-eating bull, plans to take over from me, a lion? Hah! Anyway, Schanzabeh's a good friend: it's not in his character to think up such an idea. I don't believe a word of it. The Duke of Beef scheming to do in the King of the Beasts? Rubbish! These are just lies, Dimna; lies, lies, lies, and more lies!'

'That was exactly my initial reaction, Your Majesty. I too found it unbelievable, especially of one so noble as the Duke. But then I began to wonder, "What if it is true?" And then I worried about whether I should tell you or not. "Dimna Jackal," I said to myself, "if you don't—"'

For no particular reason a loud squawk from an angry parrot suddenly cut through the air, and Dimna saw the lion's face suddenly stiffen in annoyance. They spun their heads around to look in the direction of the forest. The screeches and cries of invisibly squabbling birds rose and fell from the distant trees like a brief series of waves, then just as quickly died down, ending with two or three more squawks to punctuate the end of what Dimna assumed to be some minor domestic quarrel. The lion shook his head slowly from side to side as he turned back with compressed lips. He eased his front legs forward and stretched out with a great fanged yawn—head, neck, mane, and spine arched back into a magnificent curve. He held the pose for a second, relaxed, shook himself, smacked his lips, and lay down in the grass, resting his chin on top of crossed front paws and squinting his eyes from the overhead sun.

'What were we saying, Dimna?' he asked sleepily. 'This crazy Schanzabeh business. Seems impossible.' Softly the lion smacked his lips a few more times.

Dimna tilted his head and scratched at a flea behind his right ear. 'I agree, Your Majesty,' he said, 'but perhaps it would be wise to take precautions—just in case. Someone in your position can't be too careful.'

'Yes, I know,' sighed the lion. 'But why, Dimna, why? Why should Schanzabeh want to incite a revolt against me? Is he unhappy?'

'Apparently,' Dimna replied softly. 'The gist of the bull's speeches at these secret meetings has been to discredit Your Majesty's government. I hesitate to say it, Sire, but I understand that the Duke has repeatedly suggested that there is no reason for anyone to fear Your Majesty because you are only—forgive me—a weak coward, terrified of his great size and mighty bellow. Schanzabeh even went so far as to say that had it not been for his own good counsel to you, the kingdom

would have collapsed months ago. The Duke exhorts
his fellow conspirators to be logical and choose him as
king, since he is already the power behind the throne.'

'Oh dear, oh dear,' the lion said sadly, and he lifted
his head to rub his eyes. 'This is simply dreadful. What
on earth should I do, Dimna?'

'It would seem best, My Liege, not to be caught off
guard,' Dimna responded. 'I suggest you devise a de-
fensive strategy in case the rumours prove true. The
situation reminds me of the story of the three fishes
which I would tell did I not fear it would try Your Majesty's patience.'

'No, no, you go right ahead,' the lion said, and he
laid his head down again. 'Maybe it will help me
think,' he added wearily.

Dimna coughed politely to clear his throat and settled back on his haunches to tell his story.

The Three Fish

'Three fat fish live in a deep pool near a river bend: wise fish, clever fish, and stupid fish. They are fat because, as a threesome, they dominate their habitat. Any lesser fish that swims the channels from the river into their pool they eat on arrival. Also any newt, salamander, eel, insect, leech, slug, spider, snake, or frog who visits that pool too long, probably enters one of their bellies. And since the pool is hidden and remote, no predator ever disturbs them. That is, until one day two men who have been fishing the river accidentally discover the pool and spy these three fat ones.

The fish also notice the men. Looking up through the water, they see one man's forefinger quickly point at each of them in turn. His companion whistles softly. Delightful smiles of boyish expectation beam down from their faces. One man closes his eyes and blissfully licks his lips. The other taps his friend's shoulder and indicates where they can use their fishing nets to best advantage. He mimes casting and hauling motions over the pool. More excited whispers, then they heave their nets from their shoulders onto some nearby rocks and begin to make ready.

Wise fish acts immediately to remove himself from danger. Without even a goodbye to the others, he swims vigorously across the pool. His flashing fins and rapidly undulating body churn up a frothy wake. With great commotion he splashes up the narrow inlet towards the river and is soon out of sight.

"Effective, but not particularly elegant," remarks clever fish, quickly recovering from the shock of wise fish's sudden exit.

"Where did he go?" asks stupid fish. "Why all the fuss?"

"My friend," clever fish very slowly and patiently explains, "the men are coming soon with their nets and we must think of a way to outwit them. Otherwise they will catch us."

"How do you know?" stupid fish questions suspiciously. "Maybe these men are only fish-watchers and intend us no harm. Besides, I can swim better than a man! This pool is deep and I can hide down on the bottom."

Clever fish again patiently tries to explain the situation. "Fishing nets have weights along one edge," he says, "to reach the bottom even of this pool. And fishermen have crafty techniques for casting and dragging these nets in deep water so that large fish such as you and I are unlikely to escape. We must do something, and soon!"

"Well, I'm sure it's all very interesting," says stupid fish, somewhat annoyed at clever fish's lecturing tone.

"But I'll tell you what I'm going to do. I am going to take a nap, that's what! All this talk makes me sleepy. I don't see the men. I don't see any nets. However, I *will* sleep near the bottom—just in case. Thank you for your advice. Meanwhile, you to your way; me to mine." And with that and several dignified sweeps of his tail, stupid fish swims off into the depths for his nap.

Clever fish remains floating, alone and almost motionless. As he deliberates, he very gradually sinks. "How to act and when? That is the question," he soliloquizes. Every now and then a bubble billows from his lips and slowly wavers up to plop faintly on the surface. "I must analyze this predicament extremely carefully," he thinks. His astute fish brain reminds itself how to do this: "Systematically separate all the variables; creatively scrutinize tactical probabilities; dynamically evolve an original escape strategy." His intellect races. The more profoundly he ponders, the deeper he sinks. At last he decides to inspect the inlet from the river.

"One needs accurate information prior to formulating assumptions," he deduces as he swims. But when he arrives, he finds that the men, alerted by wise fish's noisy escape, have covered this exit with some of their nets. He swims across the pool to check the other channel. Same there: covered in nets.

"Damn," he says to himself, and begins to swim about in fear and confusion. Then he hears a splash, and turns to see a curtain of fishnet gracefully descending into the water behind him.

"Damn!" he repeats. "Damn, damn! Why did I waste so much time? This is terrible! What do I do?"

Luckily, clever fish controls this fluster by remembering one of his favourite maxims: "Panic solves nothing." Then, by way of extra reassurance, he remembers another, and, would Your Majesty believe it, even laughs as he says it aloud: "Nothing like pressure to concentrate the mind."

Sure enough, like magic, inside his mighty fish head brews a brilliant plan. He dives down quickly to the bottom of the pool. "The nets are coming! The nets are coming!" he calls out to stupid fish, who is floating in a doze.

"Oh, be quiet!" stupid fish replies, and turns away. "Leave me alone."

Clever fish bites up a huge glob of filthy old mud from the bottom and swirls it about in his mouth. It is so awful he can barely stop himself from choking. He swims back to the top and just before reaching the surface, rolls over all limp and floats as if dead, his white belly pointing to the sky.

Meanwhile, the fishermen are carefully starting their sweep across the pool, casting and swishing their nets about in the water so nothing escapes. They notice clever fish floating belly-up on the surface and haul him over. One man picks him up by the tail and sniffs him.

"Phwaaw! Eeyuuch!" he yells. "This one's dead and rotten," and flings clever fish to the ground.

With his mouth full of the dreadful mud, clever fish holds his breath as long as he possibly can. When the men are back at their work, he flips himself over and over until he reaches one of the channels beyond the net, tumbles into the water with a smacking splash, spews out the horrible mud, and rushes off to safety in the river.

Stupid fish is asleep and knows nothing of all this. He snores a thin stream of bubbles right up until the moment the net closes around him. Then he awakes to his final nightmare.

"What? What's all this, then?" he cries out in desperation as the men pull him out of the water with great shouts and whoops. However hard he struggles, there is no escape for stupid fish. The men stun him with a club, take him home to their families for an enormous fry-up. Later they tell endless stories of the "Two Big Ones That Got Away," but nobody ever believes them.'

If we choose to let conjecture run wild, then animals, our fellow brethren in pain, disease, suffering and famine— our slaves in the most laborious works, our companions in our amusements—they may partake of our origin in one common ancestor— We may be all netted together.

Darwin

The lion showed little emotion when Dimna had finished his story, but lay with his great head still resting on his front paws and his eyes closed as if asleep. The sun felt hot now, and its light shone brightly off the hairs of his tawny fur. Finally, he rolled his body slightly sideways and, unsheathing the claws from one paw, began scratching at his chin in a leisurely fashion. He looked at Dimna, stopped scratching, and sat up slowly.

'I know that in telling me this story you have my best interests at heart,' he said. 'And I understand the value of prompt action in such matters. Nevertheless, Dimna, I still cannot believe that Schanzabeh is dangerous. In all his dealings with me, he has proved good, faithful, and honest in his behaviour. So far, except for your report, there is no evidence which would lead me to change this opinion.'

'I agree completely, Your Majesty,' Dimna said. 'At present there is no evidence whatsoever. Yet I feel a need for caution. My old grandfather, may he rest in peace, drummed his favourite saying into my head when I was only a pup. "Character is what you are in the dark," he used to say. In the present circumstances that idea seems to make a lot of sense, because we don't really know what the Duke is like in the dark. We have no evidence that he *is* plotting in secret, but neither do we have any evidence that he is *not* plotting. For all we do know, his public behaviour could be an elaborate camouflage of respectability, and underneath he is a genuinely evil brute intent upon Your Majesty's downfall. Since we don't know one way or the other, it would seem prudent, at least, to beware of Schanzabeh and observe him closely in the future. There is no smoke without fire, Your Majesty. Whatever the truth of what we have heard, something is definitely burning somewhere. You must be prepared for a possible sudden attack.'

'Well, I have to admit that is good strategy,' the lion said, and he pursed his lips together tightly. 'After all, I've got nothing to lose by being on guard. And if there is any danger, then at least I'm ready for it.'

'Exactly, Your Majesty,' Dimna said. 'I feel sure that any of your loyal counsellors would agree with this decision.'

'Still,' the lion mused, 'I can't believe it possible of Schanzabeh. He appears so gentle, so soft, so good, so trustworthy . . .' The king's voice trailed off and he sat gazing into the distance across the meadow towards the river.

'Your Majesty,' Dimna interrupted softly, 'may I tell you another story, please? I've just remembered one that might be useful.'

'What? Oh, yes, yes—go ahead,' the lion said, and he continued to stare into the distance.

The Bedbug and the Flea

'One day a certain bedbug crawled into the bed of a rich man and his beautiful young wife. That night, while the happy couple slept soundly, this bedbug crept softly and gently over their bodies and sucked small quantities of blood without ever disturbing them. It soon became apparent, however, that the wife's blood had a far superior flavour. Within a week its delicate sweetness captivated the bedbug to the point of addiction; never had he tasted anything like it, and he was convinced that every night, by some extraordinary good fortune, he fed upon a sleeping angel. Life continued thus as it does for happily dazed bedbugs everywhere until one day he met a handsome flea. This flea hopped off the back of one of the rich man's dogs that passed by the bed.

"Ho ho!" he called out when he spied the bedbug hidden between the sheets. "Is this your pitch, then, mate?"

"It is indeed," replied the bedbug, "and a very good one too! And now, Good Sir, what can I do for you?"

"Well, it's like this, you see," begins the flea. "I thought I'd do a bit of exploring, you know—see the world, and stuff like that. So I'm travelling, you see—moving about and so on. And I was wondering, friend, now that I'm here, if you'd be kind enough to put me up for the night? I'd be ever so grateful."

"Why, of course you can stay," says the bedbug. "We'll feast together, too, when the humans come to sleep tonight. If you've been living off dogsbody recently, I think you'll find the young female's blood something rather special. It's a tender blood: sweet, yet with the invigorating whiff of an avenging demiurge about it—if you know what I mean. Devilish stuff, really. I'm sure you'll enjoy it."

"Well, that's very decent of you, mate," says the flea. "Thanks very much."

And so, having quickly made friendly contact, the two insects settle down in the bedclothes for an amicable conversation that seems to pass extremely swiftly, though in fact it lasts several hours. By the time man and wife arrive between the sheets, both flea and bedbug have talked themselves silly and are very hungry. No sooner does the flea sniff the wife's exquisite body-odour, her fine muskiness ravishing his senses, than his rear legs twitch convulsively and he inadvertently gives several tiny hops of quivering anticipation.

"Shh!" whispers the bedbug urgently. "We must wait till they fall asleep. Shh!"

"I know! I know!" the flea calls back. "It's just that I'm famished and she smells even better than you said." Yet he manages to control himself somewhat, and soon the couple are asleep.

Bedbug and flea now vigorously assail the delicious wife. But while the bedbug creeps about softly and gently, slipping the needle of his hollow feedtube very carefully into the wife's skin, the flea goes berserk with repeated bites that raise broad spots like pimples as red as a rose. Oh, he bites her ivory thighs and gnaws her milky breasts, he nips her delicate throat and chews her lovely buttocks and so ravenously pretty-plays her sweet carcass with his painful pinches that she wakes and feels with her fingers the awful bumps that now blemish her silky skin.

"Husband, husband," she calls out softly, and gives her snoring spouse a shake awake. "Something has bitten me! Something nasty is in the bed with us!"

"What?" he answers, still half asleep. "Bitten by a nasty bed?"

"No, no," his wife corrects him. "Vermin. Bugs. Insects. Spiders. Lice. I don't know which, but please light the candle quickly. I cannot bear this misery any longer."

Dutifully he lights the candle and calls for the chambermaid to come and help. Moments later the three of them yank back the covers and carefully inspect the bed. At the first glimmer of light, the flea takes four mighty springs and escapes right across the room without being seen. But the bedbug—ah, the bedbug is too slow and is caught skulking under a fold in the sheets.

"Aha," exclaims the husband, as he plucks him up

between two fingers. "Here's the culprit, my dear!" he says and thrusts the poor miserable bedbug under his wife's nose.

"Oh! Oh!" she cries out in shock, and bursts into a sudden flood of tears. Her husband hands the bedbug to the chambermaid and reaches over to comfort his wife.

"There, there," he says tenderly, and folds her in his arms. "It's all right, now. It's all over, my dear."

Meanwhile, none of the humans can hear the bedbug's pitiful pleas of innocence. "It was the flea; it wasn't me! It was the flea; it wasn't me!" he screeches out helplessly from between the maid's two fingers. But his cries are useless, and very soon the maid's sharp fingernails begin to press steadily into both sides of his plump little body until he splits apart in such a revoltingly messy way that it would be disgusting to describe it any further.'

*Her vomit
full of bookes
and papers
was . . .*

Spenser

'Therefore, Your Majesty,' Dimna concluded, 'just as the bedbug met his doom by trusting too much in the flea, so do I suggest that not too much credence be placed in Schanzabeh's meek appearance. He may be only a gentle grass-eater, but he is certainly smart enough to be able to find a way of inciting others, if it is true, to do his dirty work for him.'

'It's hot and I'm tired of sitting here in the sun,' the lion said, and he stood up. 'Let's move on down to Water Hole West, where we can have a drink and sit in the shade. I want to think about this a bit more before coming to a decision.'

'Certainly, Your Majesty,' Dimna said as he scrambled to his feet. 'What a good idea!'

The jackal followed the lion back through the long grass towards the main path. The king's lower jaw was stuck out in a pugnacious manner, and he moved with a firm and confident stride. For several minutes they proceeded along the path in silence. They crossed the meadow and entered the forest that swept down the north side of the valley. Huge trees with leafy heads blocked out the sun and the air was green and cool as they walked steadily along. The path wandered left and right between the tree trunks, and the ground began to rise as they climbed the natural contour of the terrain.

'I don't know what to make of this Schanzabeh business, Dimna,' the lion tossed over his shoulder.

The jackal scampered up until he was trotting beside the king.

'It is a difficult problem, Your Majesty,' he said.

'I really don't know what to do,' said the lion. 'Part of me loves him and part of me fears him. There's no middle ground between trust and distrust—no comfort, no coherence.'

'I know exactly how you feel, Your Majesty, and only wish I could have spared you this uncertainty.'

'Perhaps I should speak to Schanzabeh and see what he has to say for himself. After all, at the moment we only have some vague, circumstantial evidence against him.'

'That's true, Your Majesty, but on the other hand it might not be a very good idea to alert him to our suspicions.'

'What do you mean?'

'Well, if the Duke knows we suspect him of crimes which we admit, however unlikely, he is capable of committing, he also has time to plan a defense. We lose the element of surprise, and give him a chance to adapt to the new situation.'

'True . . . that's very true,' the lion said.

By now the trees of the forest had thinned out and the path went between clumps of thorn bushes and scrubby undergrowth that clung here and there to a rocky landscape. They emerged on the crest of a large outcrop of boulders that rose up some two or three hundred yards in a steep, undulating sweep from the grassland below. Their view across the mouth of the valley stretched for dozens of miles, and in the far distance they could see scattered herds of antelope and gazelle grazing peacefully in the noonday heat.

Below them lay Water Hole West, a natural reservoir

where the water table shot to the surface near the base of the outcrop. It was perhaps twenty yards across, enclosed on the far side by a semicircle of seven gigantic acacia trees. The near side was strewn with huge, flat rocks, partly covered in the muddy remains of different animal tracks.

A small party of elephants was relaxing among the trees, some drinking and snorting near the water's edge and others slowly rubbing their great bodies back and forth against the tree trunks as they luxuriated in the delicious pleasure of relieving sundry pachydermal itches.

Dimna and the lion surveyed this scene for several minutes before the lion remembered his thirst. He slowly lowered his body into a crouch and, contracting the huge muscles of his rear legs, sprang off the path onto a nearby boulder. In a quick series of leaps he bounded to the highest point of rock overlooking the watering hole. Shaking his mane back, he thrust his head down, bared his fangs, and announced his arrival with an almighty, thunderous roar.

The elephants below immediately froze in their tracks and turned their heads to see the lion silhouetted against the sky above. Within seconds the dominant bull raised his trunk and trumpeted an alarm. With nervous squeals from the youngsters and various irritated grunts and snorts from the females and young males, the elephants broke away from their pleasure and began moving off beyond the acacia trees. The dominant bull kept up his insistent trumpeting and ran among the slower elephants. He butted them with his great head or thwacked them across the rump with his trunk to hurry them along. Pretty soon all the stragglers were assembled beyond the trees and the herd started to troop off into the grasslands at a steady pace.

Up on the rock the lion yawned in the sunlight. He shook himself all over, and then with utmost grace bounded down the outcrop, springing easily from boulder to boulder until he came to the water's edge. Dimna followed, scampering down a twisting path with his tongue lolling out.

For several minutes they lapped up the water. Then, refreshed, they ambled off to look for a shady spot under the acacias. Presently the lion sniffed out a suitable mossy patch at the base of one tree. He sat down and faced the jackal with a very confident gaze. Dimna stood quietly to one side waiting for the king to speak.

'That water's done me a lot of good,' the lion said. 'I feel much better and am sure we can finish up this Schanzabeh business quickly. We've talked and talked so far: now is the time for action. The way I see it, we need to find out what this bull is really thinking. You're right about not questioning him too directly. We may alert his suspicions and give him time to adapt his story. What do you say to the idea of trying to infiltrate his organization, assuming, of course, that there is one? Do you think you could help me with this, Dimna?'

'Of course, Your Majesty,' the jackal answered. 'However, there may be an even easier way to determine Schanzabeh's guilt or innocence.'

'How's that?'

'Put it this way, Your Majesty. I know the Duke pretty well and he trusts me as much as anyone. Give me a bit of time, and I'm sure I can draw him out. He's bound to let some clue drop if he's implicated in this affair. I'll question him indirectly, and will find out the truth no matter which way he turns to evade me. Before I'm through I'll know whether he is sowing dissent or not, how many other animals are involved, and what their plans are.'

'That sounds pretty good,' interjected the lion.

'When I've learned these details,' Dimna continued, 'I'll report back to Your Highness and bring the Duke with me. You'll be able to interview him and see for yourself whether he's involved or not.'

'That's excellent, Dimna!' the lion exclaimed. 'But how will Schanzabeh give himself away if he is guilty?'

'By his eyes, Your Majesty. He'll not dare to look you in the face. His gaze will be shifty and he'll appear worried; the pen of his heart will write all his thoughts on his forehead. His normal cheerfulness will be replaced by an uncertain manner, and he will generally behave suspiciously. If he is guilty, Your Majesty, he will clearly give himself away—you can count on it!'

'That makes sense, Dimna, because if Schanzabeh is innocent, there will be no reason for him to behave in this way.' The lion paused and turned to wipe his mouth against one of his shoulders.

'Okay,' he resumed. 'You go to Schanzabeh and talk to him, then bring him back to me. Meet me this evening by the tree in Banyan Field. Let's get to the bot-

tom of this nonsense once and for all. Off with you,
Dimna, and be quick about it.'

Dimna left the king at a gallop and cut back across
the plain. He climbed to the fringe of forest that crept
down into the mouth of the valley until he spotted the
gently meandering river beyond. It seemed part of a
giant silver serpent that lay peacefully uncoiled along
a greenish floor, its tail slithering miles back towards
blue mountain foothills, its head hidden behind the
contour of the valley's opposite slope. The jackal took a
bearing on a particular grove near where Schanzabeh
usually spent his day, and headed diagonally downhill
at a steady trot.

In half an hour he was close enough to hear the gur-
gle of the river's steady current. He came through a
screen of very tall reeds and catkins where the water
curved off upstream in a long, southeastward sweep
through flat mudbanks. Inside this crescent, after the
tall stuff, sweet, edible grass grew thick and delicious.
It was the Duke of Beef's habitual grazing ground and,
except for a few infrequent antelope, other animals
tended to respect his privacy and pretty much leave
him alone.

Dimna moved on upriver along the curve until, sure
enough, he caught sight of the great bull ruminating
under a shady tree. Schanzabeh lay on his side with
his forelegs tucked up under his body, chewing over
his morning feed and shooing flies off his haunches
with lazy whisks from the brush of his tail. The jackal
approached slowly, looking glum.

When Schanzabeh saw him he said, 'Why, Dimna—

this is a pleasant surprise! I haven't seen you for days. I was beginning to wonder whether you were deliberately avoiding me.' The Duke of Beef struggled onto his knees and made ready to stand up.

'Good afternoon, Your Grace,' Dimna said, and he stopped and raised a front paw. 'Please don't get up on my account. I didn't mean to disturb your rest.'

'Not at all, not at all,' said the bull, and heaved himself onto his legs. 'I'm delighted to see you. How are things?'

'Oh, as well as can be expected under the circumstances,' the jackal replied, looking away. 'And you? You seem well.'

'Yes, yes, feeling very fit indeed. But what's the matter, Dimna? You don't seem yourself. Are you in some trouble? Tell me, for I am the natural one to help you, being already so much in your debt.'

'Thank you, Your Grace,' the jackal said, and he flicked a look up into the bull's eyes and then turned his head away again. 'That's very kind of you, but you see . . .' and here he paused and let out a long sigh. 'Well, it's not myself I'm worried about, to be frank.'

'Come, come,' said the bull. 'Whatever the cause of your sadness, let me be the one to help you transmute it into happiness. Here—sit yourself in the shade beside me and we'll talk about it.' Schanzabeh settled himself into his former position under the trees, and Dimna, with a resigned shrug of his shoulders, squatted down on his haunches nearby, his head hung low.

'No one has seen you at court for many days,' Schanzabeh remarked pleasantly. 'I asked others if they had heard of your whereabouts, but no one knew anything. Even The King was curious.'

'I'll bet he was,' Dimna snapped.

'What do you mean by that?' the bull asked, inclining his head to catch Dimna's downcast eyes. 'Have you had some quarrel with the lion? Is that the trouble?'

Dimna shook his head. 'No, no,' he said. 'It's just that I prefer my freedom away from the court, that's all. Especially after what I have heard,' he added mysteriously.

'And what have you heard?' asked Schanzabeh.

'Certain disagreeable things about the lion's character that make me wince more than if I had stuck my snout into a pot of hot mustard. He may be The King, but he's still a type of cat, you know. Cats are unpredictable, spiteful creatures—more so than I would have ever believed possible.'

'This is dangerous talk, Dimna,' Schanzabeh observed. 'You're obviously very upset and not thinking clearly. Stop being so obscure and tell me what's bothering you.'

'It's not easy, Your Grace, it's not easy,' the jackal said, slowly shaking his head from side to side. He pursed his lips and sucked in a long breath. 'Do you remember the promise I made you the first time we met?' he asked.

'Of course,' Schanzabeh answered. 'How could I forget?'

'Well, it's still true, you know,' Dimna continued. 'I feel a great affection for you, my friend, and even though we haven't seen each other for some time, you're often in my thoughts. I'd still do anything in my power to protect you from harm.'

'Thank you, Dimna; but this flattery, while it's nice to hear, is getting us no nearer to understanding the cause of your unhappiness.'

'I know, I know,' Dimna said. He briskly rubbed his eyes with a paw, suddenly stood up and paced about. 'It's not me I'm worried about, you know. It's you!'

'Me? How can that be? I'm perfectly all right, I assure you!'

'You're in danger, Duke,' Dimna said, stopping directly in front of him. 'You're in danger from The King. That's what I'm trying to tell you.'

'Oh, come on, Dimna, this is nonsense. Why, only yesterday evening the lion and I went for a stroll together. We had a very amicable conversation. How can I be in any danger from The King?'

'Exactly because he *is* The King. You don't know what I know. We should tremble with fear in his presence, for we are always under his power. One courts a thousand dangers by becoming a royal favourite, not the least of which is The King's whim. Even the most honoured can topple in the flashing of a gnat's eye. The highest places are the most dangerous to climb, for a fall is seldom survived.'

'These are truisms, Dimna, that everyone knows. But I don't think they apply in the present situation. I've caused The King no offence nor threatened him in any way which could make him want to harm me.'

'I know, and that's exactly the injustice of it all,'

Dimna said. 'That's what bothers me so much. Here you are, a loyal subject and royal counsellor, doing a good job as everybody knows, and The King . . . The King . . . oh, these cats are such ungrateful creatures! I have no faith left in anything. Let madness reign and chaos triumph! The hell with it all!'

'Dimna, Dimna, calm yourself. These outbursts are getting us nowhere.'

'Look,' said Dimna, 'you must never forget that The King is a carnivore and you are a herbivore. At any moment he chooses, you can become his food!'

Schanzabeh shifted his position uncomfortably. 'Of course I am aware of the difference in our diets,' he said, 'although I seldom think of it in quite such dramatic terms. After all, the lion and I, not to mention the other meat-eaters in his kingdom, have coexisted in harmony for some time. Why do you bring this up now?'

'Precisely because of what I heard recently about the lion's preparations for his mother's birthday party next week. He intends you to be the feast of honour!'

'What?' exclaimed Schanzabeh, and he scrambled to his feet so rapidly that the ground shook and a small cloud of dust rose up into the air. A shudder ran over the bull's body and he stared at Dimna in amazement.

Every animal in the kingdom knew how dear to the king's heart the queen mother's birthday party was; for all the lions it represented the major social occasion of the year. The Royal Pride, comprising many of the dowager lioness's children, grandchildren, and great-grandchildren, gathered together in a strictly family affair to roam the kingdom's borders, hunting and feasting all day. Several visiting relatives from neighbouring territories—cousins, aunts, uncles, nieces, or nephews of the king—attended the function as well. It was therefore very important that everything run smoothly. To ensure the hunt's success, the king sent out in advance his fleetest-footed leopards to drive suitable game back towards the hunting party.

It was a long-standing law of the kingdom that accredited vegetarian citizens of the lion's territory were immune to attack from any meat-eater. This special hunt, like any hunt by flesh-eaters, was confined to nomadic or migrating prey on the borders, or the occasional edible stranger unlucky enough to be caught trespassing. In this manner law and order were maintained in the kingdom. A greater variety of animals, each with its own social habits and special abilities, were able to live together in relative peace and harmony. Traditionally, the king himself always made the first kill for his mother's birthday party and presented her with the carcass amid raucous growls, grunts, roars, and even little purrs of admiration from the various leonine onlookers.

While it was true that Schanzabeh was a distinguished citizen of the kingdom, it was equally true that technically he was a stranger to the area, not having been born there and, indeed, the only animal ever to have been domesticated. But it was tradition that worried the bull more, for it was imperative that the lion, being king, make an impressive kill, something substantial enough to get the party rolling by providing meat for everyone. Although Schanzabeh had lived in the valley for a long time now, he had not yet been there for the queen mother's annual birthday party. Furthermore, game had been sparse for all the carnivores during the past few months. While it was a subject in which Schanzabeh naturally took little interest, he was, nevertheless, informed about this situation, having overheard numerous flesh-eaters—even the king on one occasion—talking among themselves about how difficult it was to stalk down a square meal these days. Certainly this year it was not going to be easy for the leopards to flush out a kill worthy of their king.

All these many details gradually filtered through the bull's mind as he listened to the jackal complaining about the maliciousness of cats in general and the king's treachery in particular. Although Schanzabeh's common sense told him it was absurd to distrust his friend the lion, Dimna's argument nevertheless grew increasingly convincing as he yapped on and on in righteous indignation, playing upon the bull's innermost fears with a steady stream of antiroyalist abuse. Schanzabeh stood uneasily, towering over Dimna and nervously shifting his weight from one foreleg to the other in a jerky rhythm. Soon his feelings became so confused and his perceptions so unclear that he proved an easy target for the jackal's manipulation.

Schanzabeh felt trapped. He had the uncomfortable feeling that he was reverting to his former status of a captive beast of burden hemmed in by uncontrollable circumstances and doomed to plod out his life towards an unavoidable end. Things seemed even worse now, for at least when he served the merchant of Distawand there had been some measure of security, someone who took an interest in his safety and well-being. Now he was abandoned and alone, merely another domestic animal trying against the odds to survive in the wilderness. If what Dimna said was true, his position was hopeless. No one could help him escape the murderous intentions of the lion, and when Schanzabeh realized this fact, his spirit crumpled. A low, rasping moan of resignation heaved up from the depths of his body. He stopped moving and stood absolutely still as if in a trance, shocked to the roots of his being. An involuntary shiver rippled the skin along his backbone.

For a moment Dimna thought he had gone too far, so sudden and utter was the abjectness that visibly overcame Schanzabeh. 'Come, come, my friend,' he said. 'I've reported what I've heard to warn you, not to discourage you. My news is hardly good, but at least you can now take steps to protect yourself. What do you think you'll do?'

Schanzabeh's eyes were glazed over and his attention drifted miles away in a vacant reverie. After several seconds he gave a start and focussed on the jackal before him.

'Why?' he asked, just louder than a whisper, 'why has The King's opinion of me changed so drastically?' He coughed and snorted uneasily, trying to find more voice. 'What have I done for him to use me so severely?' Schanzabeh swung his head to look intently left and right, then continued. 'There must be court intrigue behind this sudden change of heart. Some enemies are determined to get me into trouble with the lion. Such a bad impression of me will already have been created in his eyes by these backbiters that, no matter what I do in future to please him, like the story of the cormorant and the star, he will only assume I am faking. Do you know it, Dimna? Do you remember the story?'

'No, I can't say that I do.'

'All right,' said the bull. 'Just a minute. It's short. Listen.'

The Cormorant and the Star

'There was once a cormorant who caught sight of a star's reflection on a gentle sea. Thinking this slowly wavering patch of light was a fish, he dived underwater and tried to catch it. Of course the cormorant failed, yet stubbornly he continued to dive again and again, believing that by effort alone he must eventually succeed. In the end he grew so angry and frustrated that he swore never again to dive after a fish.

From then onward, even though he suffered extreme hunger on a meagre diet of small crabs, shrimps, and shells found along the shore, the cormorant refused to dive after any fish, for he assumed it was as impossible to catch as the star on the water.'

Living starts when you start doubting everything that came before you.

Socrates

127

'Surely The King has committed a similar mistake,' concluded Schanzabeh. 'How else can one explain his ingratitude for my past service? He has believed some slander circulated against me by worthless courtiers, and now that his suspicions are aroused, feels no qualms in taking my life.'

'Well, I have to admit that theoretically you could be right,' Dimna said casually. 'But personally, I doubt it: you're much too gentle and popular a figure to incite such invidious mudslinging. Can you name even one animal—let alone a whole group—that you feel does not have your interests at heart?' Dimna smiled up at the bull for a moment to allow the question to sink in and then continued. 'No, sir, I think your basic goodness and kindness are carrying you too far in seeking a way to exonerate The King in this. After all, *he* is the one who plans to kill you, and for taking that decision *he* must be held at least partially responsible. I say he is motivated by his own bad nature, which is capricious, ruthless, and sadistic. He is jealous of your many good qualities because they so markedly contrast with his own deficiencies. Furthermore, he possesses the power to strike out and destroy anyone he dislikes without fear of punishment. How like a right royal cat that is! It *pleases* His Majesty to contemplate your destruction! *God's teeth!* I lose control whenever I think about it!'

The jackal's hackles rose in a bristling ruff over the back of his neck and across his shoulders, and on stiff legs he bounded quickly around the bull several times with his lower jaw jutting out and upper lip curled back to display sharp, yellow teeth. He shook his head vigorously from side to side with an infuriated snarl and cast fierce glances up into Schanzabeh's eyes. The bull watched, waiting for his friend to quiet down. He flicked his tail at a hovering cloud of flies that were annoying his rump. Dimna's seizure gradually wore itself out; he veered off to one side and lay down in the grass, panting furiously.

'I'm sorry about that, Your Grace,' he said with a gulp. 'Please excuse the outburst.'

'That's all right,' said the bull. 'Forget it.'

A gentle breeze rustled the leaves of the tree over-head, the water of the river burbled in the background, the bull's tail swished through the air and slapped at buzzing flies bold enough to risk landing. Gradually the soft pant-pant-pant of Dimna's breathing sub-sided. Out of nowhere a tick bird swooped down under the tree and settled on the bull's back, hopped about, and rummaged under his coat for blood-sucking prey. Schanzabeh turned his head and gave the bird a friendly look, then started chewing his cud in a thoughtful manner.

'Oh, okay, then—I may have exaggerated a bit,' Dimna admitted at length. 'But you've got to do some-thing, Schanzabeh! I also came here to give you a mes-sage that was passed on to me. The King expects to see you early this evening at Banyan Field. You must be prepared for that meeting!'

The bull nodded his head in silent acknowledge-ment.

'Of course logically,' Dimna continued, 'we both

could be wrong in our explanation of his behaviour. One could begin with different assumptions.'

The bull looked at Dimna. 'Yes,' he said, 'I've been thinking that too.' He shifted his body around until he was facing the jackal. The tick bird jerked its head upright, quickly checked that everything was safe, vigorously ruffled and smoothed its feathers and then went back to work. Schanzabeh chewed slowly five or six more times, then swallowed and carried on as follows:

'We could assume that The King is ill and suffering a temporary mental aberration. Or maybe I have committed, as I did when I first arrived in this valley, some unwitting affront which has so grieved His Majesty as to ruin our friendship. Finally, I suppose, one could simply attribute his change of mind to the mysterious inevitabilities of destiny. Certainly if it is my fate to be killed by the lion, then I shall accept God's will, knowing that even an innocent death can be part of His plan. Personally, however, I stand by my own interpretation that there is a court conspiracy. I cannot name anyone, but our court is full of anxious animals whose hearts are bursting with envy at seeing me so much in The King's favour, who cannot help but practice mischief to bring me down. Fruit trees risk having their branches broken, canaries are caged because they sing prettily, and peacocks cry out when their beautiful tail feathers are plucked. So it is that a king's favourites are frequently destroyed through no fault of their own.

'I am sure The King is just and will enquire before

punishing anyone. He is my friend, and will not delight in my suffering. I do not believe him to be deliberately malicious, no matter what you say. Yet his own feelings towards me can be only too easily switched by rumours and insinuations circulated to undermine my position. The effect of repetitious slander is no less certain than the action of dripping water on a stone; even the hardest surface is imperceptibly worn away. Therefore, neither my own efforts to establish my innocence nor the goodwill of The King will help me against the machinations of secret enemies. This point is made clear in a story about another lion and a camel. In order that you may better understand my mind, I'd like to tell it to you.'

Schanzabeh paused for a moment, snorted to clear his throat, and then proceeded with his story.

*The Camel,
the Lion, the Leopard,
the Crow, and the Jackal*

'There was once a remote road which twisted through some mountains and skirted along a ridgeline above a wooded valley wherein a lion ruled as king. Among his advisers were three crafty creatures who fed off his leavings, namely, an elderly leopard, a jackal, and a crow.

Now this particular lion—a powerful hunter—wished to be considered honourable and just. He never neglected his duty of providing for those weaker than himself. He developed a keen sense of justice and always sought to do the right thing, even in a crisis.

One morning a long caravan of camels passed along the road and kicked up a huge cloud of dust that hovered for hours over the lion's valley. And when the tinkling of their bells had finally receded in the distance towards the world of men, a young, pitiful straggler could be seen flopped down on the rocky verge. He was exhausted and wide-eyed from fear at his abandonment, his owner—one of the caravan's merchants—having shared out his load among some

132

other camels and left this weak, stumbling one behind. For a long time he lay stretched out along the ground, breathing heavily, hardly able to move. At length, however, he managed to stagger to his feet and, with an even looser-jointed amble than is normal for his kind, careened down in a drunken manner from the roadside to the much cooler forest below.

This young camel was leaning against a tree, wondering where to find some chewy grass to eat, when the lion suddenly appeared. Expecting nothing but to be devoured, he attempted to save his life by humbly making the only offer he could.

"Help me, O Powerful and Tawny One—help me, please," he cried out. "I am weak and utterly alone. Lend me thy mighty protection so that when I am recovered, I can repay you with devoted service."

The lion immediately took pity on this feeble one-humper, the likes of which he had never seen before. His patriarchal instincts to offer refuge were fully aroused.

"What manner of beast are you?" he asked. "And what is it you think you might be able to do for me?" He paused to look inquisitively into the camel's huge brown eyes while the latter quivered at being so near what he supposed was the brink of death. The lion noticed his fear and moved back a pace.

"Not that it matters," he said soothingly. "You don't have to bargain with me for my protection. I don't believe that I should limit myself to performing only those acts which are directly in my own interest. I was just curious to know what you might have in mind. I'll help you in any case—whether or not you can do anything for me."

"Th-thank you, you're v-very k-k-kind," stammered the camel. "I can see th-th-that someone as strong as you are has little n-need for someone as weak as I." He paused briefly to collect himself and then continued with greater confidence.

"I am a beast of burden, Sir—a humper of goods for men, a vegetarian called camel. Yesterday in the mountains I was eating some bright green thornberries which I was too young to recognize as poisonous. When my master caught me, he beat me, and the other camels—even my mother—called me fool, but already it was too late. My sickness began as sharp blasts of pain which grew like those rough gusts of wind that precede the desert sandstorm. I fainted briefly and could move no more when the final whirlwind struck deep within my guts; they transferred my load and left me on the road above. Now I stand feebly before you. What I can do for you is uncertain, for I am as ignorant of your habits as you are of mine. But I can tell you this: no one will be more devoted to you for the kindness you have shown in simply listening. I thank you as one living beast to another. Do with me as you wish." He bowed his head and knelt, but the lion begged him to rise.

"This forest and its surrounding fields are my realm and I am lion, King of Beasts," he said. "You are welcome here and have my personal guarantee of safety. No one will dare molest you, therefore go about your business in peace. Come—let me show you to a nearby meadow where you may feed and a stream from which to drink."

And so, in next to no time, the camel recovered his health and grew sleek and fat-humped. Most of his days were spent eating, resting, and socializing with other friendly animals in the territory. Aside from infrequent errands requested by the lion, the camel had no duties to perform. Everything proceeded as smoothly as dew down a leaf until one day the lion was wounded by a huge bull elephant during a hunting expedition. By the time he limped back to his den, he was weak from loss of blood. There was nothing to do except rest and hope that somehow he would survive. Like any other wild animal he fasted for several days, concentrating his strength. His eyes grew bright and his stare intense. He let his mind drift blankly down the flow of time, for he could feel that inner calm increased proportionally to his detachment. Meanwhile his dependents—the crow, the leopard, and the jackal—grew very hungry indeed. The lion eventually noticed their condition and took pity on them.

"Look," he said, coming out of his restorative reverie, "just because I'm incapacitated doesn't mean you three have to mope about half-starving. Surely old leopard here is able to hunt up a few tidbits to keep you going until I've recovered my strength."

The crow rustled his wings and shot a quick glance to jackal's briefly lifted eyes. They both knew that leopard, however beautiful the rosettes that still dappled his splendid coat, was simply no longer an efficient hunter. Oh, he *tried* for several days after lion's rather pointed suggestion, but . . . well, he couldn't *really* make a go of it. There were a few scrawny guineafowl, the odd anteater or skinny monkey — but nothing you could really call a meal, especially once it was shared among three. Slowly but surely, the leopard, the crow, and the jackal began to waste away. And things hardly improved when lion announced he wished to break his fast; now their slim pickings had to be shared with him as well, and as king he naturally enjoyed first choice. It was not long, therefore, before leopard called a private meeting with crow and jackal.

"I must mention," he said, "something which has been on my mind for many days. Here we are struggling to survive while among us that wretched camel thrives. Where is the justice in this situation? He is not even of our fraternity, being an eater of vegetation rather than meat. He is, in short, but an overfed stranger who, however pleasant a personality, contributes very little to our community. What say we kill and eat him? He's so big and fat that, even after subtracting His Majesty's share, there'll be enough of him to keep us going for more than a week."

"The idea is excellent," commented jackal drily, "and hunger pleads much in its favour. However, I am afraid you are forgetting that our noble leader, like a good many creatures of power, is rather enchanted with the concept of projecting a clean image to posterity. It is simply inconceivable for him to view himself outside a role of the most unsullied honour. Surely you remember his promise of protection to our delicious-looking friend? History would judge him odious if he now retreated from his word. Certainly he will veto your suggestion, and you would be an utter fool, in my opinion, to believe otherwise."

"Why, you snotty little carrion crawler," hissed leopard. "Have you got a better idea, then?" he snarled, leering forward ominously, fangs bared.

"Now, now!" crow cawed loudly. "Come, come, gentlebeasts," he said. "It does us no good to argue among ourselves—none whatsoever." He ruffled his feathers, shook himself smooth, and hopped from one foot to the other in a bouncy little dance that distracted their attention.

"It so happens," he said, once he'd settled down between them, "that I may well be able to reconcile your different attitudes. It won't be easy, but with your permission I am prepared to try. The highly nutritional potential of leopard's idea cannot be denied, and yet, to be sure, jackal is absolutely correct in his assumption about the king's most likely response. But what if the unsavoury fact of camel's death is packaged and delivered in such a way as to be acceptable to lion? It's all a question of proper presentation. If you're prepared to wait here peacefully for a while, I shall fly immediately to the king and try to sugarcoat this pill. What say you, then? Are we agreed? No more bickering while I'm away?"

"Yes, yes," said leopard and jackal in unison. They well knew crow was the cleverest in presenting anything to lion. "We agree."

"All right, then," said crow, "see you soon," and he launched himself into the air and flapped over to King

Lion's den. Putting on a starved and meagre look, he made a profound reverence and, puffing ever so slightly with pretended exertion, said, "May it please Your Majesty to hear me a few words?"

The lion had been dozing, but was filled with expectancy at seeing the crow, for it had become this black bird's routine to wing over on those occasions when leopard made a kill. "Oh, my belly—be prepared; good news, by God's will," he said to himself. And to crow he said, "Say on, Master Corvo," for such was his name. "Speak what is in your mind. How goes the hunt? What is the menu today?"

Blushing like a black dog, crow set a good face on the matter and answered boldly (for he knew what was likely to come). "Sire, I'm afraid our claws are bare and, as it were, the menu is blank. Old leopard is not the hunter he once was, and as a result we're almost all famished to death. He simply lacks the speed to catch what he could in his youth. And as he weakens with each day that passes, so do things go from bad to worse. Thus, Your Majesty, I cannot report meat for today. Leopard missed his pounce upon a young piglet which jackal and I were helping him to stalk. However, despite this unwelcome news, Your Majesty's three servants have put their heads together and found a remedy for our plight, and, if Your

Majesty will but give them leave, have contrived how we shall enjoy a feast."

"A feast, you say? How? What's your idea?"

"Well, and here I hesitate, Sire, for I know that what I am about to suggest will deeply sting Your Majesty's heart. I proceed, nevertheless, for it is sincerely what we advise." Crow paused to take a deep breath, and, looking bashfully away from the lion's gaze, continued.

"To put it bluntly, Sire, we want you to condone the death of camel for the sake of Your Majesty's life. He is round, plump, fat, and full as an egg. Dead he will serve Your Majesty better than alive."

"What?" roared the lion, and with a front paw thumped the ground in outrage. "You dare to suggest that I break a solemn promise? You vile bundle of stinking feathers—get out of my sight before I tear you to pieces!" He began a mock lunge forward, but his wound froze him with a jolt of pain.

"Hoouuu! Aww!" he quavered, and, screwing up his face in agony, gingerly lay back down. Crow obediently retreated a few steps and braced himself for another flow of hot words.

"If it weren't for that damned elephant you'd probably be dead by now," grumbled lion after he'd opened his eyes. "You miserable beast of wickedness, I ought to—"

"With respect, Your Highness," interrupted crow, "without 'that damned elephant' we would have no problem, and I never would have made my suggestion. As it stands, 'that damned elephant' is likely to prove the death of both of us, not to mention many others."

"Bird, shut your beak!" snarled the lion. "Say what you will, nothing in your faithless sophistry will ever lead me to violate my word. You can heap up shallow pretexts and cunning fallacies into the most splendid edifice of treacherous argument, yet never will I enter in your evil trap! Can you not see what you are asking? Am I to snatch back the gift of safety? Rescind my hospitality to creatures in distress? Camel has never in the slightest degree excited anyone's displeasure, and yet now, prodded by selfish hunger, you see him as a meal and not a friend! Oh, leave me, leave me; I weary of this game."

"And if I leave, Your Majesty, then soon we both shall leave this wretched scene by death, and after we are starved away, what then of poor friend camel? Your kingdom gone and chaos reigning, who will save him from marauders bound to come? Camel will lie dead and stripped of flesh by hunting wolves or slavering jungle dogs, or even, dare I say it, another lion who holds no promise like your own. What then, O King? Throw our lives away, yes—camel, jackal, leopard, and I are but your slaves—but keep your own, My Liege, I beg you from the knees of my heart, keep your own life or dissolution follows, especially for gentle camel and all other creatures in your land."

"I will not do it!" declared the lion emphatically. "No matter how you build your words, I will not allow you to kill camel!"

" 'Kill,' Your Majesty? Did I say 'kill'? Caww, now at last I see what has trapped Your Majesty in the good-

ness of his royal heart. No, Sire, killing is not the way;
we are not taking a life, it is being donated! Please let
me prove this to Your Majesty. Camel will come here
with all of us and Your Majesty will hear him volunteer
his death. I promise what I say is true. Leopard, jackal,
camel, and I have decided Your Majesty's survival
precedes our own; we are ready, as it were, to be destroyed for our own safety. Hence my visit. I only
wished to warn Your Majesty of the nature of our business when we come."

"Get out of here," lion said quietly, "and this time I
mean it." He bowed his great head in fatigue and anguish, and after a long sigh added, "Your trim tale has
put me in a foul temper and I want to be alone."

"Certainly, Your Majesty," said crow as he with-
drew. "I apologize for upsetting you. Please forgive
me." Crow flew quickly to the other two and found
them asleep on the ground.

"Wake up, wake up!" he cried, and when they did he
told them all that had passed in conversation with the
lion.

"So if you'll follow me in my plans," he said at the
end of his report, "I'll tell you how we go. Are we three
now agreed? Are you two with me?"

Leopard and jackal looked briefly at each other and
then nodded their heads.

"Affirmative," said leopard.

"Ditto," said jackal.

"Good," said the crow, and he strutted about between them for a moment, seemingly lost in delibera-
tion.

"Okay," he said at length. "Here's how it'll be. Jackal, in a minute I want you to fetch our fat morsel. Tell him The King is starving, and that in duty to His Majesty we three propose to go and surrender ourselves up as food to prolong his royal days. Tell him it's merely a formality, but we wondered if he would care to accompany us by way of expressing gratitude for our lives of peace and plenty under good lion's reign. Got it?"

"Yes," said jackal, "I understand."

"Fine," said crow, "that's great. I'm sure you'll succeed very easily. But now hear me out. Come closer, for this part of the plan is for your ears only."

Leopard and jackal huddled forward with crow, and all anyone outside their circle could have heard was whisper, whisper, whisper. Soon jackal shot off to find camel, and it was not long before the four beasts together made their way to the king.

"Your Majesty," said crow to the exhausted lion, "we your servants are most powerfully moved by the sight of Your Majesty so greatly weakened. It deeply ails us that Your Majesty's most precious life might perish from famine and, though I am miserable at how little-worthy I can offer Your Majesty, yet with willing mind I present this feeble body. Take and feed, My Lord, of this my poor and simple carcass; die not for hunger—make me a meal. The consequence to public good of Your Majesty's best health outweighs my puny life." And here he waddled humbly forward to prostrate himself at lion's feet and stretched out his neck, lying still as death.

The leopard no sooner saw the crow flat on the ground than he slinked smoothly up and gave the bird a kick in the tailfeathers. Crow, giving a loud caw of pain, fluttered off to one side, looking very annoyed.

"Crowmeat for a king?" leopard asked. "Why, nothing could be worse for anyone, Your Majesty. That filthy fowl is hardly fit for worms: eat him and you'll feel worse, not better. And look here, Your Majesty: you need a meal, not a mouthful of dry bones and feathers. Have some real meat, then, Sire—eat me!" And leopard followed crow's ceremony and lay upon the ground before the king, offered his neck and waited.

"Wait a minute, wait a minute," yapped jackal, stepping forward. "This will not do, Your Majesty; his flesh will prove tough as old tree trunks, and impossible to digest. I have as much true sense of duty as I hope does any loyal subject. Hear me, then, when I say that, though I am smaller, my youth makes me more tender. Bite leopard to break your teeth, but if you want flesh for food—bite me!" And here he too lay down while leopard hissed from short retreat.

"Caw!" shouted crow as he hopped down from a rock and pranced up. "No way, Your Majesty, no way! You can't consume dogsbody; it's not safe. More tender than leopard, yes—I grant you. But fit for lions? Never! Jackal flesh stinks to high heaven; and even fresh it is putrid." Jackal swung his head around and glared sideways at crow in a most annoyed manner.

All this scene stirred camel's emotions into suggestible confusion. The dynamics of group pressure tugged him steadily towards conformity. He did not wish to be left out of the action any more than he wished to displease the lion. So he felt it perfectly safe and only good manners to plod forward once jackal had moved aside.

"With respect, Your Majesty," he began, "but I am many times larger than all these other three combined. And my flesh is neither foul nor tough, but in fact by many considered delicate and sweet. None of the earlier objections apply in my case; I am truly many meals fit for a king. Please, Your Majesty, save your life: eat me up and suck my bones!" And likewise he lay upon the ground and stretched his neck towards lion.

Contrary to expectation, however, after a brief pause crow was heard to say, "You know, I think he's right. Don't you?"

"Yes," said leopard as he sprang, "camel flesh is dainty." And he sank his gripping claws deep in camel's neck and tore open his throat before that poor beast had chance to breathe another word. Jackal and crow rushed in to lend some helpful nips and pecks— and all this while, of course, lion looked the other way.'

'Poor camel!' Dimna said, as soon as he realized that Schanzabeh had finished his story. He noticed the motionless tick bird standing with its head cocked, quizzical, as if expecting more. The bird shuddered violently into a feathery blur, shook smooth, and resumed pecking parasites. 'Poor camel,' Dimna said again.

'Yes, indeed,' said the bull. 'Perhaps now you understand why I trust so little my chances against a determined conspiracy. Any offense by me will merely confirm the slander The King has heard, making him that much angrier and more dangerous. Yet defense, because the lion is naturally quicker and better armed than I, offers meagre hope as well. Oh, dear, why is everything so deadly complicated? I cannot find a plan. Do you have any ideas, Dimna?'

The jackal sat up. 'Well, I think you're quite right to avoid an immediate confrontation,' he said. 'But if direct aggression seems imprudent, you can still resort to a little subtlety. You need to think like a warrior who faces an enemy stronger than himself. Calculate a devious strategy. Your only advantage is the element of surprise, therefore you must be prepared to strike the first blow fiercely if the situation warrants it. If you intend to slump up to the lion like a ready-made victim, then I think your chances of survival are slim and, frankly, you deserve all you get. You must beware small, threatening hints in the king's behaviour, changes in posture and suchlike, that always signal any attack in advance. If they materialize you must stand firm and communicate clearly by your own stance how determined you are to brook no nonsense, trusting that the lion will back down and allow you time to explain your innocence sufficiently to pacify him. You will have to judge whether he's going to listen to you or not, and if not, then you'll have to act quickly and charge him at full power with your horns.'

Dimna looked up into the bull's eyes, and Schanzabeh shuffled on his hooves nervously. 'That's my advice,' the jackal concluded. 'I hope you are prepared to follow it. If not I fear you may end up like the sea when it raided the sandpipers' nest. Do you mind if I tell you the story?'

'No, no—not at all,' answered Schanzabeh, shaking his head from side to side in a worried manner. 'It's only fair that you reciprocate,' he added politely.

The Sandpipers and the Sea

'A pair of sandpipers lived near the sea. One day the female said, "Nesting time is here again! We need to prepare a place for our young."

The male looked over at her, recognizing his responsibility, but reluctant to make too much effort. "Okay," he said, "this will do. We can scoop something out in the sand behind this tuft of grass. It'll act as a bit of a windbreak, and camouflage you as well."

"The hell with the wind," squawked his mate. "It's the sea I'm worried about. We need to move farther inland or the high tide will reach my eggs."

"The sea can't reach you here!" retorted the male. "It's perfectly safe, I assure you."

"Don't fib to me about safety," said the female. "You had better be sure about events before making rash promises. Too much loose talk and you'll end up like that turtle who hitched a ride with some geese."

"What happened?" asked the male.

"Listen and I'll tell you," she answered, disdainfully tossing her head.

"Oh, all right," he said, settling himself down onto the sand and wiggling about until he was comfortable.

Chitchat Turtle and the Geese

"For many years a pair of geese lived by a wonderful pond with a friendly yet garrulous turtle named Chitchat. One summer, however, there came a dreadful drought which reduced the pond to a veritable puddle and made life very miserable indeed for the three friends.

The geese decided to leave, went to the turtle and said, 'Look here, Chitchat, things aren't what they used to be. The place stinks with rotten mud, the weeds tangle our legs, and there's but puny food left in this dying mess. Sorry to leave you, but we're flying off to a lake we know up north where life might be more tolerable.'

Chitchat looked very hurt and said, 'That's all very well for you creatures with wings, but what am I supposed to do? When the water goes, so do I, for on dry land I'm as helpless as a beached whale. What to you is simply a detail of comfort becomes for me a matter of life and death. Please spare me this agony of hopelessness and figure out a way to take me with you.'

The geese conferred briefly together, and after a few

quiet quacks returned from their huddle and the gander spoke as follows:

'Dear friend, there may indeed be a way in which we can move from here as three. The method, however, involves deadly risk to you if silence you cannot keep. I must say this bluntly: you talk too much. Our greatest worry is you'll waste our favourite turtle if you speak a single word during our trip. No matter what happens, you must keep quiet to stay alive.' The gander paused for emphasis, stretched his neck and shook himself in a blur of ruffled feathers, flapping his white wings and waggling his tail before settling down again.

'What can I say?' Chitchat began softly a moment later. He hung his head, the skinfolds around his neck drooping pathetically. 'Of course, you're quite right about this personality trait: restraint in speech has never been my forte. Gabblers like me so adore random talk that we forget how fatal twattle often proves. Thank you for the frank reminder; I'm very grateful for your advice.'

The turtle looked up with a wry grin and lurched closer by two steps. 'If life saturates the pool of silence,' he declared, 'I must drink its calm waters. I swear by my shell, by the lids of my eyes, and the sixteen webs between my toes that not another syllable will I utter until we reach the northern lake you seek.' With that Chitchat shut his mouth firmly.

'Good!' said the gander. 'We can start immediately. Just follow my instructions and everything will work out. If you are truly enough of your own friend to keep mum, there will be no danger to your turtlehood. But now excuse us, please, as we need to go and find something.'

The geese waddled off and returned carrying a strong stick which they dropped near Chitchat's feet.

'Snap your beak around the middle of that,' said the gander. 'Hang on tight and we're ready to go.'

Chitchat clamped on to the stick as directed. Goose and gander each gripped an end in their own beaks and, with several mighty flaps of their wings, lifted themselves and the dangling turtle into the air. At last the three friends were headed north towards the lake. During their flight, however, they passed over a village and were noticed by some of the yokels below.

'What's that cartwheel in the sky?' shouted one as he pointed at the strange sight.

'Look at those geese with the stick!' yelled a small farmboy.

'It's a turtle! It's a turtle! It's a funny flying turtle!' cried a little girl, whirling around in an excited jig of joy. Soon a great commotion arose, everyone rushing to view nature's incredible threesome and shouting with all their might.

'Shut up, you pesky humans!' Chitchat yelled back, forgetting the price he must pay for exhausted patience. 'God pluck your eyes out, you blithering clunkheads!' he shouted as he plummeted to earth and was smashed to smithereens. That night several villagers enjoyed turtle soup for dinner.''

Never try to teach a pig to sing: it wastes your time and annoys the pig.

Mark Twain

150

"A very good story, my dear," the male sandpiper said
when his mate had finished, and he rose from the sand
and bobbed towards her. "Yet believe me when I say
that the sea is too wise to challenge us openly. Nest
here and be not afraid: I will protect you."

"But how can you compare yourself to the sea?"
screeched the female. "You're just a little bird!"

"Nevertheless," continued the male calmly, "I'm not
as helpless as I might appear. The sea dares not behave
unkindly, for he is afraid of the consequences. He is a
considerable strategist, and always examines the remote results of an action."

The female gave up under the barrage of such intel-
ligent-sounding nonsense, and in sputtering exasperation finally laid her eggs in a scratched-out hollow behind the tuft of grass. The sea, however, had overheard
the male sandpiper's boast, and was curious to know
what he would do. Accordingly, after several days had
passed and observing that the nest was momentarily
unattended, the sea, rolling his billows far up the
beach, snatched the eggs under his watery skirt and
swept them away to some hidden dry spot in a cave.

"Now look what's happened!" screamed mother
sandpiper when she discovered her loss. "And what
are you going to do about it, big-beak?" she demanded
of her spouse. "You who talked such huge, strong
words!"

"Just watch me, please," answered the male in an
untroubled manner. "I'll either get our eggs back or
revenge us on the sea. Don't worry; I'll keep my promise." He flew off quickly to talk to all the other birds in

the neighbourhood, who were indeed outraged at the calamity.

"If we fail to claim justice from the sea," the sandpiper said, "his boldness will increase and none of our offspring will survive. Unless you join me in making a formal protest to the Supreme Council of Birds, extinction is our lot! We must stop this danger now!"

And so it was that a great peeping caucus of shorebirds rose up into the air and went to make formal complaint. They flew off to the mountain abode of the Most Mightily Winged Ones and were admitted, finally, by fierce-eyed eagles of enormous size. The sandpiper bobbed forward and made an impassioned speech that echoed squeakily throughout the chamber. He addressed the Phoenix, who perched above the rest, smouldering in brilliant colours, elected power for the day, his fire feathers rippling menacingly.

"Most Perpetual Featherness," the sandpiper began. "Command the power of this timeless council to attack the sea for stealing my young. Bring your mightiness to bear and boil him off the planet. Use fire, My Lord, to scorch him into ineffectual steam. If ye represent not mere figureheads of strength, heed my plea and swoop with us against this child molester."

A vote was taken and the Supreme Council agreed to enforce its will. Now the shorebirds were joined by a limitless squadron of terrifying air creatures. There were Phoenix, Simurg, Dragon, Anka, Griffin, Garuda, Roc, and Pteranodon—each multiplied into a thousand million forms too horrific to contemplate. The sea saw them coming in a huge darkling cloud and stilled his

waves in terror. The mighty voice of all the birds and
their gods and their ancestors rang out: "Give back the
sandpiper his eggs or be burned into the sky!" And in a
flash of watery silver that
streaked up the sand,
the sea did exactly as he
was told, even gently
rolling the eggs right
back into their nest
by the tuft of
grass. Lady
Sandpiper
never doubted
her hus-
band's word
after that.'

Dimna breathed the last word with a smile, briefly closed his eyes, then opened them to watch the bull nodding his head in silent agreement.

'Your story is certainly most apt, Dimna,' he remarked, idly pawing the ground in front with his right hoof. 'I appreciate the practicality of your advice about taking necessary precautions. However, I think the best thing for me to do is appear before the lion with a clear conscience, untroubled and unoffended. I do not wish to aggravate his suspicions further by behaving too defensively too soon. There is a slim chance that if The King sees me being my normal, positive self, he'll remember our true friendship. But at the same time I'll not forget your warning to be ready for an attack if there appears to be no hope for a reconciliation.'

Schanzabeh turned his head and looked over at Dimna. The jackal rose slowly on all fours, stretched, and vigorously shook himself. With a flurry of quick, rearward kicks he sent a brief shower of dirt, grass, leaves, and pebbles arcing off behind. Then he trotted over to the bull and looked up.

'That's fine, Your Grace,' he said, 'but allow me to give you one final piece of advice as a watchword. Beware if The King stares steadily into your eyes, flattens his ears, or begins to lash his tail about. Study carefully the position of his paws and watch out for any sudden tension in the muscles of his haunches. If he makes any two of these gestures you may be sure that he is about to pounce, and Heaven help you if you are not ready to meet him like the worthy champion I know you to be. If he sees you standing steady and imperturbable, he may check his attack and listen to you further. But frankly, I doubt it; you had better be ready for the worst.'

'Thank you, Dimna,' Schanzabeh said. 'I'll bear those points in mind. It's getting late and I think I had better be on my way to meet the lion and face whatever destiny has in store for me. We all know how cheap a life is, so if I am not to see you again, Dimna, I want you to remember how rewarding it's been for me to know you.'

'Oh, but Duke,' Dimna cried out, 'I want to come with you to Banyan Field! Please let me be with you during this difficult moment.'

'Well, that's very kind, but I don't want you to get into any trouble on my account,' responded the bull. 'Just because I'm in the lion's bad books is no reason for you to end up in them as well. No, I think it's best if you stay behind, Dimna.'

'Let me come partway,' the jackal pleaded. 'I can't bear to see you go off on your own.'

'Okay, partway, then,' the bull relented. 'But please leave me when we arrive at the edge of the clearing. I must make the final approach alone. It's getting late. Let's go.'

Schanzabeh slowly began to move off towards the trail that led northeastward to Banyan Field and the Tongue, and Dimna followed behind. This time the tick bird recognized that it was more than a mere shift of position and quickly flew away. Soon bull and jackal left the grazing land and proceeded upriver following a flattened path through eight-foot-high kiang grass.

They moved between two rustling screens of greenish-yellows, the bull lumbering steadily ahead and Dimna trotting in the rear. The afternoon sun blazed low in the sky, its light raking across the landscape and scattering all detail into glinting brilliance. A zephyr caressed the iridescent kiang tips, swaying them back and forth, one into another, in brief, shimmering waves. Schanzabeh's horns, wider than the trail, ploughed through its undulating sides, and to Dimna, following so much lower down, it seemed he was momentarily lost in a rippling tunnel of shadowy grass where distant light magically flickered deep into his eyes.

Once they reached the edge of Banyan Field, the narrow trail led into more open territory. Schanzabeh stopped at a point where they were still invisible to anyone in the clearing.

'I'd be grateful,' he said, 'if you would leave me here. I wish to spend some time alone before approaching The King.'

'Of course,' said Dimna. 'I quite understand. Good luck, then, old friend: I hope to see you soon!'

'Thank you,' said the bull. 'You've been very helpful.'

'Goodbye,' said Dimna. As soon as he was out of Schanzabeh's sight he broke into a run along the perimeter of Banyan Field, cut left down another path, turned right at Flat Rock, and continued as fast as he could on the shortest route to his brother's den. As he had hoped, Kalila was dozing away in a patch of sunlight outside the entrance. Dimna flung himself down on the ground beside him, and, panting furiously, tongue lolling out, gulped, 'Wake up, brother . . . wake up. . . . Good news at last. . . . Hurry!'

Kalila rolled over with a long yawn and opened one eye suspiciously. 'Oh, it's you, is it?' he said. 'Hmm,' he sniffed, and rolled back to his former comfortable position, obviously savouring those last vanishing delights of fading sleep. 'Why are you in such a lather?' he asked at length, with his eyes still closed.

'Schanzabeh and the lion,' gasped Dimna. 'They're going to fight, you can bet your whiskers. Come and watch. Hurry!'

'What!' demanded Kalila as he leapt to his feet fully awake. 'What are you talking about, you evil sneak? What dirty tricks have you been playing now?'

Dimna grinned and winked mischievously up at his brother. 'Come on,' he said, standing up. 'There's no time to go into detail. We'll miss the climax. Follow me and be of good cheer. Things will work out; you'll see.' He trotted away without looking back.

Kalila raced after him, keeping pace shoulder to shoulder. 'What are you talking about?' he repeated. 'What's going on?'

'Stop fussing and let's move!' snapped Dimna. He took off in a fast run that led them all the way back to the edge of the field. They both flopped into some long

grass and lay there for several minutes panting in unison. Off to the left, maybe two hundred yards away, they saw the lion sitting under the shade of the big old tree which gave Banyan Field its name. A leopard, a couple of vultures, a boar, a wolf, and some other smaller, less identifiable courtiers appeared to be keeping the king company as usual. Schanzabeh was nowhere to be seen—presumably still somewhere off on their right, meditating prior to his entrance.

'This is it,' began Dimna, when he had recovered enough breath to speak. 'The fang and horn fight of the century! On our left, wearing the mane and tawny coat, Lion—King of the Beasts! And on our right, hidden for the moment, but due to appear at any second, wearing horns and hooves, Schanzabeh—the mighty Duke of Beef!'

'You're crazy,' said Kalila.

'This event comes to you right in the convenience of your own backyard thanks to the sterling slick and sly promotional efforts of Dimna—that famous superstar of subterfuge, sabotage, and psychological manipulation. This is the Big One! One of these two great contenders is going to leave his skin behind! But hang on just a moment, folks. We've still got time for a few choice words of wisdom from my distinguished colleague here. Over to you, Brother Kalila!'

Kalila sat up stiffly on his haunches. 'Your megalomania appears to be approaching clinical proportions,' he said calmly. 'One feels it is dangerous even to talk with you, much less criticize your behaviour. The softest hint for caution gets blown away like smoke in the wind. To offer you sensible advice is as useless as it was for the busybody bird that tried to help an ignorant ape—'

'A story, folks!' interrupted Dimna. 'He's going to tell a story. Oh, goody-goody and lucky us!' He jumped up and whirled around several times, yipping gaily and chasing his tail.

'Yes, I am, you loud-mouthed dimwit! It's unlikely that my efforts to instil even a smidgin of common sense in you will have the slightest effect. Yet you are family, and I am determined not to abandon hope. So sit down, shut up, and listen!'

Dimna stuck his tongue out at Kalila but held his peace.

The Apes and the Busybody Bird

'A troop of apes once lived contentedly enough on the wooded side of a mountain, gathering fruit and nuts, roots and grubs, and other apish things to eat. But when the winds of winter came suddenly one afternoon, these apes grew cold and miserable and huddled together shivering and chattering away for all they were worth.

Now one of them is just a bit cleverer than the rest, and when he spies something bright and curious in a nearby bush, he leaves the group and goes to investigate. It is a glow-worm, but this smart young ape thinks it is a spark from which he can make fire and keep warm.

Accordingly, he bats the glow-worm out of the bush on to the ground and heaps dead leaves upon it. These actions attract the attention of the other apes, and they troop over amid a great gabble of gibberish to see what's happening. From up in a nearby tree a bird screeches out:

"Hey, you apes—you can't make fire that way! That's a luminous larva—not a flame. It won't work! It won't work!"

The apes ignore this unwanted advice and begin to help their brother by gathering sticks, twigs, grass, and more leaves to pile on the pitiful glow-worm. Meanwhile, the first ape, growing colder, gets down on his hands and knees and blows vigorously into the bundle, hoping it will burst alight. Some of the others stand around rubbing their chests and bellies and actually holding out their palms towards the imaginary warmth.

This is too much for Busybody Bird. He flaps down from the tree and lands right beside the huffing and puffing ape.

"Listen, you big monkey," he scolds, "I'm telling you that you can't do it that way. Don't you realize that you're dealing with a phosphorescent insect, *Lampyris noctiluca*, commonly called a glow-worm? It's not possible to start a real fire with a shiny bug."

Big Ape stops his blowing and slowly swivels his head around to face this nagging know-it-all. Without a word he reaches out and grabs Busybody Bird by the neck and yanks him over. Then he slowly twists the astounded bird's head off.'

The analogical form can evade the categorizing of our rational thought and reach other sectors of the mind.

Dr. A. J. Deikman

'I am most deeply touched by your abiding faith in my consistent worthlessness,' Dimna remarked quietly, when Kalila had finished his story. 'Such patience deserves a righteous reward, and if not now, certainly in the life hereafter.' He turned his head and sniggered into his shoulder.

'You wretched dungheap of sarcasm,' spat Kalila, lunging forward with a growl.

'Now, now, sunshine,' leered Dimna, 'let's not get carried away.'

'Carried away! Why, you snaggle-toothed horror— what in hell are you talking about?' began Kalila. 'You're the one who's engineered some deliberate calamity here! How you did it and what it is, I don't know and don't want to—but one thing's sure: it's bad news for Schanzabeh and the lion, not to mention the rest of us. Carried away! Why, you miserable personification of envy—look who's talking! You haven't been carried away: oh, no! You've been ... you've been ... whooshed off in a typhoon of jealousy ... overwhelmed by a whirlwind of lust ... hurled in a hurricane of avarice! Greediness for fame has snatched your tiny hopes, and eagerness for wealth holds them hostage! You're a slave, Dimna—a slave to noxious passions! Who can call you brother when your only love is self?'

'Hold it there, please,' said Dimna, 'if you don't mind.'

'What is it?' snapped Kalila.

'Well, nothing really,' said Dimna hesitantly. 'You're doing terrifically. I certainly find your vituperation most instructive. But tell me. Isn't there another story that might be appropriate at this juncture? A little something for our edification? You know—a tale that summarizes, as it were, the situation we have before us. What was that you were saying? "A slave to noxious passions." Yes, that's it! Very good! Very good! Reminds me of a fable along a similar theme. There's a vigorous punchline that goes: "Deceitful companions are worse than madness." Yes, yes . . . and the title . . . let's see now . . . "Sneaky and the . . ." "Sneaky, the Tree, and . . . " It's on the tip of my tongue . . . a story about humans . . . '

' "Straight!" ' exclaimed Kalila. ' "Sneaky, Straight, and the Tree." '

'That's the one!' said Dimna. 'Why don't you tell it? Who knows—it may even have a beneficial effect on my character.'

'You're mocking me, you little villain,' said Kalila. 'I ought to bite your ears off.'

'Oh, come on,' said Dimna. 'Stop your yapping. What's the matter? Don't you remember the story?'

'Of course I remember the story!'

'Wonderful!' said Dimna. 'Get on with it, then. I'm all ears, but to your bark, not your bite.'

'Ha ha,' said Kalila. 'Very funny.' He glared into Dimna's eyes for a long moment, then curling his upper lip, he swung abruptly away with a snort of disgust, stomped off three or four paces, turned and stomped back. 'Okay,' he said. 'Sit down and listen.'

Sneaky, Straight, and the Tree

'Two humans, Sneaky and Straight, were equal partners in business who travelled around the country dealing in this and that. One day Straight found a sack by the roadside containing one thousand gold coins.

"That's the end of this trip," he declared gaily, when they had finished counting the coins. "We can go home and live it up for three or four years without having to work. Aren't we lucky?"

"We are indeed," answered Sneaky. "How observant it was of you to notice the sack and investigate."

So the two partners joyfully headed back to their village to celebrate their good fortune and begin their life of ease. When they were nearly home, Straight stopped under a huge old tree and said, "Let us sit here in privacy and divide the coins—five hundred to you and five hundred to me. Then we can each go our separate ways and enjoy the splendour to which we will soon grow accustomed."

"I think it would be a pity to disband our association," Sneaky said. "We were united in poverty, so why not now in riches? Fortune appears to smile on us as a team; what's the point of splitting up when things seem to be working better than ever? Personally, too, I think it would be a mistake for us to appear suddenly wealthy. Why tempt with envy those terrible spongers we both know among relatives and friends? No, I suggest we each withdraw a hundred coins for immediate expenses and secretly bury the remainder under this tree. Later, as we have need, we can return together, dig up the sack, and make joint withdrawals."

Straight thought this was an excellent idea. They executed this plan and went to their respective homes. But that night Sneaky returned and stole the remaining eight hundred coins, taking care to smooth over the ground and leave no trace of his digging.

After some months of very pleasant living, Straight realised he was nearly broke. He went to Sneaky and explained the situation, indicating that he needed to call upon their hidden sack of gold.

"You must be psychic," Sneaky said. "I was just about to come and see you for exactly the same reason. Yes, yes, let's go to the tree. I too need money!"

Of course, when they dug up the ground there was nothing anywhere. Sneaky soon began to manifest extreme anguish.

"Oh! Oh!" he cried out, tearing at his hair. "Is nothing sacred in this world? How could you betray me so underhandedly? I always thought you were my friend, but now this!" He beat his breast and rent his clothes, crying piteously, "How could you? How could you?" And he drew back in seeming horror, staring at his partner incredulously as if he were a demon.

"What are you talking about?" Straight demanded indignantly. "I didn't steal anything! It didn't even occur to me! You must be trying to fob off your own crime on me, you villainous wretch!"

Back and forth their brawling flew with increasing vigour. In the end they stomped off to the local magistrate and made loud, formal complaint, each against the other. This sage judge immediately perceived that such an obscure matter would not be quickly sorted out. Accordingly, he threw them both in jail to calm down. Five days later, he took statements from the two partners and asked if either had corroborative evidence. Straight answered that there was nothing but his own word to back up his side of the story: he had no documentation. But Sneaky said, "In fact, Your Worship, I have a witness who can verify my accusation. It is none other than the Spirit of the Tree under which we buried our treasure. Ask the tree for the truth!"

This claim, of course, quite astounded the magistrate, but he decided to say nothing and simply await developments, hoping that time might prick out the core of the matter. In fact, he released both partners on bail for the night, instructing them each to appear by the old tree early the next morning. As soon as Sneaky had posted his bail, he hurried off to find his father.

"Dad," he said after reassuring the old boy that he was all right despite his stay in prison, "I'm in a bit of trouble and need your help."

"What is it, son?" asked the fond parent.

"As you probably know," Sneaky explained, "I've had a fight with my partner and as a result he's trying to cheat me out of money that is rightfully mine. What's particularly irritating is that this sum represents savings I had specifically set aside for you and Mother in your declining years. That dirty Straight has gone and stolen a secret cache of gold we hid together—taking my share as well as his own. My only witness is the tree near where we originally buried the treasure, and that's where I need your help."

"What do you want me to do?" asked the concerned old man.

"It's a lot to ask," answered Sneaky, "but I'd like you to go tonight and hide in the middle of that old tree. It's hollow and you'll be able to shinny up inside with little trouble, but please do dress warmly. Tomorrow morning when the magistrate and his official appear to question the tree, make sure you speak out against Straight."

This devious plan appealed to the old man's own cupidity and, unable to resist his son's honeyed words, he went off under the cover of night to hide as requested. Very early the next morning the magistrate and various dignitaries, worthies, and elders of the village appeared by the tree, together with Sneaky and Straight. After duly reading out the formal charges against both partners and briefly elaborating upon their earlier sworn statements, the magistrate himself swore in the tree as a witness.

"O Spirit of the Tree," he cried, "do you solemnly swear to tell the truth, the whole truth, and nothing but the truth, so help you God?"

Everybody strained forward to listen for any response. Way up inside the old tree Sneaky's father disguised his voice and hollered down in wavering tones, "I dooooo!"

Naturally enough, everyone looked at everyone else with some considerable astonishment after these words, hoping to confirm by various smiles, nods, grimaces, winks, whispers, and mutterings their relative sanity. But there was no doubt about it, they agreed; the tree had spoken.

"Very well," intoned the magistrate once order was restored. "It is alleged by the partners that eight hundred gold coins were jointly hidden among your roots on such and such a date. It is further alleged that at some time since, one of these partners returned, dug up, and stole this treasure. Who did it?" There was a long pause during which everyone kept very silent. Then the same peculiarly quavery voice issued again from the tree:

"Straaaaight stole the gold! Straaaaight is crooked and a thieeef! Heee took the coins!"

"Thank you," said the magistrate. Then, turning to Straight, he asked, "Do you wish to cross-examine the witness?"

"Yes, I do," said Straight. He inspected and examined the tree, discovering the hollow up—'

'Hold it a second,' interrupted Dimna suddenly.

'What is it?' asked Kalila with distinct annoyance.

'Schanzabeh,' Dimna said, and he flicked his nose twice towards the right. 'The main event is about to start.'

Sure enough, the Duke of Beef could be seen emerging from the long grass which screened that end of the clearing. He moved slowly yet steadily into the open, keeping his eyes to the ground.

'I have almost finished,' Kalila said coolly. 'To continue . . . '

'Not now!' Dimna snapped in exasperation. 'Are you blind?'

'May I remind you that this story was your idea in the first place?' Kalila insisted. 'Now that I've begun, I intend to finish.'

'Oh, for God's sake, if you must,' spluttered Dimna. 'Hurry up then. So get on with it.'

'I will,' said Kalila with steely composure. And he did.

'Straight walked around the tree and discovered the hollow up its middle. Saying nothing, he gathered a bundle of dry firewood, twigs, and leaves, stacked them in the hollow and lit a fire.

"I protest, Your Honour," Sneaky cried out. "What is the meaning of this outrage? The defendant is threatening the witness!"

"Not at all, Your Honour," answered Straight. "I'm merely attempting to entice a louder and more distinct answer from our Spirit of the Tree. My methods will produce results very soon, I assure you."

"Objection overruled," intoned the magistrate. "Proceed."

A few minutes later, when flames were licking up the inside of the tree and sending out great billowing clouds of thick, acrid smoke, Straight yelled out, "O Spirit of the Tree! Can you hear me?" There was a brief silence followed by muffled coughing, spluttering, gagging, and choking sounds, then screams.

"*Aiee, aie, aie!* Quick, quick, quick! Water, water! I burn! I smother! Help, for God's sake! Help!" And Sneaky's father tumbled out from the tree, black, smoking, and on fire. His hair was gone and there was the awful stench of seared flesh, but nevertheless some people couldn't help laughing. Very soon he died on the spot, whimpering piteously.

"Here lies the true Spirit of the Tree," declared Straight. Sneaky burst into tears at the unexpected death of his dear old dad, and fully confessed his crime. The magistrate sentenced him to immediate death by hanging from a branch of the old tree, declaring loudly for all to hear, "Deceitful companions are worse than madness!" The fire was put out, and later the eight hundred gold coins that were discovered in Sneaky's house were awarded to Straight.'

When Kalila had finally finished this story, he sat down carefully at some distance from his brother. Dimna hardly noticed his aloofness and seemed to care even less; for several minutes most of his attention had followed Schanzabeh. The bull was now within twenty yards of the banyan and offering cheerful greetings to the lion, who sat against a dangling backdrop of aerial roots, his head framed by the regally ruffled mane.

Yet, although they could distinguish not a single word, the jackals heard unmistakable tension in Schanzabeh's rumbling voice. His body sagged with an obvious perturbance of heart. When he attempted an obeisance, dropping briefly to his knees with lowered horns, the movement looked heavy and awkward. The king's responses were gruff and curt; his pose appeared to stiffen. Dimna knew his pestilential counsel played heavy with the mood; suspicions flowered from burrs left prickling on the mind.

Faster than a blink the lion crouched and sprang. Schanzabeh bellowed readiness to meet his snarling king. One of his horns nicked almost a quarter-ton of hurling cat. The lion yowled in spitting rage, spun, and rushed the bull's flank, slashing great bloody streaks in living steak as he clawed up swiftly onto the back. Deep down in flesh his talons sank; his fangs gripped hard around an ear.

'Whuuooarh!' roared Schanzabeh in agony, and he charged across the field, twisting, bucking, turning—anything to fling off the wounding hug.

'Whee-heagh!' cried Dimna. 'Will you look at that? We've cracked it!'

'Shut up,' snarled Kalila. 'You villain!'

Schanzabeh gallops back from the distance, heading straight for the banyan. Leopard, boar, vultures, wolf, and tinier thunderstruck courtiers scatter in a frantic scramble of fur and feather. The bull slams his body into the curtain of banyan roots, trying to scrape off the clinging lion. But it's no good, so he begins banging his and lion's head against a thick branch until lion, finally too dazed to hang on, slumps off and only just misses a berserk goring by scrambling into the protective tangle of roots.

So ends the first round. In a fury Schanzabeh charges the banyan tendrils again and again, but too late: lion has escaped to the other side of the shielding tree. With a loud groan of pain and frustration, the bull shakes free his horns and backs away to catch his second wind, eyes glinting with frenzy. For several minutes both combatants gulp air with great rasping heaves. Blood spurts from the stump of Schanzabeh's bitten-off ear; the king has hardly any spit to lick that gash along his side. But soon the battle starts again.

Lion creeps out to act as target, taunting the bull to charge a dozen times and more, always eluding horn and hoof by deft rolls and pirouettes, until bull is tired again, so very tired he stops, stands still for gasping breath. Then lion begins his attack, for now bull is target. So it goes for many rounds, back and forth between the two, but in the end it's lion, designed to kill, who clamps his death grip on Schanzabeh's wincing muzzle. For a moment of dizziness the landscape teeters between lion's clench and bull's wrench. But there is no more air for life in Schanzabeh: the king has blocked all passage. Bull is suffocating and his world begins to spin as in an endless dream. He shudders, gurgles, and topples over, while lion jumps to avoid the crashing body but never loosens grip. In minutes Schanzabeh is dead.

King Lion proclaims victory with a great, final roar that shakes terror in the sky. He springs onto Schanzabeh's carcass and shouts, 'Meat for carnivores! Come and get it!' Then, wounded and exhausted, he staggers down and, after a few uneasy steps, keels over in a faint.

'My son! My son!' cries the queen mother, who, along with probably every other creature in the kingdom, has rushed to watch the ending of the vicious fight. She races into the clearing, motherhood's incessant cares bursting forth in crisis. 'Oh, my poor boy,' she says, 'my poor boy,' and begins to kiss, lick, and nuzzle her bedraggled and inert offspring. Various courtiers appear and begin to bustle about trying to look official and efficient. Orders are shouted; there is much movement to and fro as crowds of beastly spectators stream onto the field to congratulate the victor (or his mother), stare at the dead bull, or simply gawk blank-mindedly at one another. Finally the king opens his eyes and feebly lifts his head, obviously in a state of shock. He turns left and right in a vacuous, slack-jawed gape until he suddenly collapses against his mother's shoulder. A great cheer erupts from the crowd.

'Long live The King!' shouts Dimna from the sidelines. 'Long live The King!' And he begins whirling around in a little jig of victory when . . . *wham*, Kalila suddenly tears up from out of nowhere and violently bowls him over. 'What th—' manages the sprawling jackal, but his outrage lasts only seconds for Kalila's teeth are all over him until Dimna the Damnable yips from pain and goes limp with surrender. Old smooth-talker is shocked speechless at finding himself flat on his back, straddled by his angry, mean-looking brother.

'One move and I'll rip open your windpipe so fast you won't know what hit you,' spits Kalila viciously. 'You're the vilest piece of dogshit anyone's ever had the misfortune to meet on this planet. Throwing away the life of a friend and risking that of The King! Why, you treacherous hypocrite—who can trust you now? I don't know what you've done, but I've seen the sickening results. It's unsafe to know you. I don't want you as a brother. I disown you! Consider our relationship severed asunder: we are divorced! From now on, don't even speak to me!'

Kalila pauses for a moment to catch his breath and collect his thoughts. 'Listen, you piece of wicked flesh,' he says at length. 'This is positively our last encounter. 'I'm going to tell one final story, and then you'll never have to listen to me again.'

'Thank God for small mercies,' Dimna mutters into his whiskers.

'Quiet, devil!' snarls Kalila, and he quickly snaps his teeth on cheeks and ears until Dimna whimpers from pain. 'This story's for me, not for you, you lousy bonebag!' Kalila growls, stepping onto Dimna's shoulders to hold him down.

'Whether you like it or not, it belongs here, and I'm damn well going to tell it. Maybe you'll understand why I'm giving you up, but if you don't—well, too bad! So just lie still and shut up, or sure as I'm breathing you'll be a dead jackal, brother or not—I don't care.'

Kalila glares into Dimna's eyes with acute intensity. Then he begins to tell his last story in a soft, even, and very determined voice.

The Iron-Eating Mice

'There was once a rich young trader who went off to do
the deal of his life in a far country. Before he left, however, as a hedge against losing everything during his
trip, he deposited a couple of tons of iron with a friend,
reasoning, quite rightly as it turned out, that the price
of iron would never fall and that, whatever happened,
he could always come home to this little nest egg and
start again.

The deal of his life flopped completely; he returned
some years later virtually bankrupt. In order to raise
cash he went to his friend and asked for his iron, as he
wished to sell it. His friend, having a year or so earlier
been caught tight in a web of debts, had already sold it
for his own benefit.

"Oh, at last!" he said. "I am so relieved to see you.
I've been worried for months. Something dreadful has
happened and I didn't know how to contact you."

"What is it?" asked the trader, already sniffing the
beginning of some fraud.

"Well," said his friend, "you remember how we
stored all your iron in that locked room at the back? I

had no idea the place was infested with mice: hundreds of them, it appears. I'm very sorry to have to tell you, but your iron is completely gone—devoured by the wretched creatures! They ate your iron!''

Now, this young trader knew better than to blurt out the obvious accusation. His agreement with his friend was purely oral; there were no receipts or contracts, and he wished to avoid any protracted legal arguments. There's more here than meets the ear, he thought to himself. Let it unravel a bit further and maybe we can pick up an end and yank forth the truth.

"Eaten by mice?'' he said aloud. "Oh, no—not *that* again! It's already happened a number of times in my career. They just don't make iron like they used to: nowadays it's so sweet and soft. The foolish man who supplied me probably anointed it with one of those so-called rust-inhibiting oils which made it extra tasty for our little furry friends. Probably slipped down their throats like syrup. Still, one mustn't grumble; I'm alive and have my hands to work with. One must take these little setbacks in one's stride. Ha ha!''

So delighted was his friend by this easygoing attitude that he immediately invited him in for lunch, hoping that under a lather of abundant hospitality the unfortunate incident might be permanently forgotten. Host and guest passed an agreeable afternoon carousing and drinking together in a splendid display of comraderie. When it came time to leave, the guest managed, once outside, secretly to kidnap his host's only son and heir. He led the boy home and locked him safely in the cellar.

Next day when the trader was about his business in

town he met his friend, who was looking terribly distraught. "Good heavens!" he exclaimed. "Whatever is the matter?"

"It's my son," groaned the other man wretchedly. "He's been missing since last night. We've looked everywhere, but so far there's not a single clue."

"That's funny," remarked the trader. "Now that you mention it, I remember seeing a small boy in the distance yesterday evening when I left your place. He's blond, isn't he? Yes, yes—it could well have been him. He was being carried off by a sparrow hawk. It was gripping him by the hair with its talons and flying away into the sky."

"What are you talking about, you liar!" exploded the other man. "My son carried off by a sparrow hawk? That's preposterous! I ought to punch you in the—"

"My dear friend," interrupted the trader. "Calm yourself, *please*, and do be reasonable! In a town where mice can gobble two tons of iron, what's so remarkable about a sparrow hawk carrying away a little boy? I wouldn't be surprised if one flew off with an elephant!"

Now the other understood the game was up, and that the trader was not the fool he had supposed. He hung his head and confessed. "Be not angry," he said, "for the mice didn't eat your iron."

"Be not sad," replied the trader, "for no sparrow hawk kidnapped your son. Pay the value of the iron and take back your boy."

So it was agreed, but the two men never spoke to each other again.'

Kalila stepped from Dimna's shoulders, paused for
one final look down, and then, turning away and
walking off, said simply, 'That's it. Now get out of my
life!'

Dimna scrambled to his feet and shook himself vigorously. After a malicious glance in his ex-brother's
direction, he sped off to see what was happening elsewhere. Specifically, he went to find the king.

By now it was nearly dusk, and the clearing was free
of spectators and aimless stragglers. A mixed crowd of
scavengers—various hyenas, jackals, weasels, vultures, buzzards, and others—was busy tearing, pecking, gobbling, and chewing their way through the free
meal which had been Schanzabeh. An angry cloud of
insects buzzed about overhead, impatient for a chance
at the leftovers. The stench of slaughter was everywhere and what was left of the bull was barely recog-
nizable. Meanwhile, the lion had recovered himself
sufficiently to dismiss his mother and limp back to
some privacy under the banyan. The blood of battle
had been licked clean from his fur, but he was alone
and looking very morose when Dimna tiptoed up very
cautiously.

'Am I disturbing you, Your Royal Highness?' the
jackal whispered softly.

'What?' said the lion tonelessly. Only his amber eyes
moved as he sought the source of interruption among
the evening shadows. 'Oh, Dimna. No. What a day.'

'I apologize for not appearing sooner, Your Majesty. I
got held up and couldn't make it before the bull.'

'What?'

'My report, Your Majesty. My detailed report on
Schanzabeh's treasonous activities. Although I suppose it's a bit late now.'

'Yes, a bit late now,' repeated the lion. 'That's true,'
he sighed, and looked away and snorted loudly.
'That's very true.' He hung his head and made several
very unhappy noises deep in his throat.

'Is there anything wrong, Your Highness?' Dimna
asked gently.

'Oh, Dimna,' choked the lion in the softest, quietest,
most private torment possible, 'Schanzabeh! Schanzabeh is dead! The nicest, kindest, gentlest, wisest,
most honest and wonderful friend that I ever had—virtually my other self—and I killed him. Cruelly and
without mercy! I could munch my paws for sorrow.'
The lion's body shook under a burst of awful sobbing.

'There, there, Your Majesty,' said Dimna, and he
nuzzled a supportive nose against the king's shudder-
ing shoulders. 'Take it easy, please, Sire. Calm down.'

For several minutes the king spent his grief in
Dimna's presence. Then, when he had begun to regain
a grip on himself, when his woe only surfaced in the
occasional sniff or sob, the jackal spoke as follows:

'Your Majesty, everyone knows how difficult it is to
be king. Leaders have a tough job, and the worst part is
avoiding tenderheartedness. But Schanzabeh was a
subversive, Your Majesty—the ringleader of a determined conspiracy to bring you down! I give you my
most solemn oath that this is true. I interviewed him
very carefully as we agreed, and Your Royal Self witnessed his most guilty behaviour. Would an innocent

KALILA
AND DIMNA

beast have challenged you so? No, I say! So please forgive yourself, Your Highness. In weeding out so dangerous an enemy from the realm, you performed but an elementary duty. Better traitor dead than revolution spread! Now I think, if I may say so, Your Majesty, that what you need is rest. Everything will seem much clearer after a good night's sleep. You've had an extremely active day.'

'Yes, I suppose you're right,' said the king, and without any more ado he parted from Dimna and went to take this advice. And while some did, others did not live happily ever after.

*But
enough of this;
there is
such a variety
of game
springing up
before me
that I am
distracted in
my choice,
and know not
which way
to follow.
'J is sufficient
to say,
according to
the proverb,
that here
is God's
plenty.*

Dryden

Reality,
in fact,
was only a
background
to a fairy
tale . . .

Greene

IN BETWEEN

"Incredible!" King Dabschelim said, when Bidpai finished telling this version of *Kalila and Dimna*. They
faced each other in the wavering light of half a dozen
thick, beeswax candles which servants had lit at dusk
nearly four hours earlier. "That is certainly the longest
story that I have ever heard anyone tell in one sitting,"
continued the king. "You must be exhausted!"

"I am fairly tired, Your Majesty, as a matter of fact.
But no more than yourself, certainly: after all, you've
been listening all the while."

"Nonsense!" said the king. "I've been entirely pas-
sive, and what a delight it has been to listen to you.
Truly wonderful. Yes . . . now what about something
to drink or some food? It's late, and you must be
hungry."

"No, thank you, Your Majesty. If you don't mind, I
think I'll go straight to my bed."

"Certainly," said Dabschelim. "Yes, of course," and
he rose to help Bidpai up. "Come, take my arm." Bidpai gratefully accepted the offer, for he was indeed feeling faint after his marathon.

"Guards!" shouted the king. "Chamberlain! Someone come and help this man!" There was a flurry of footsteps in the corridor, and a moment later Bidpai felt himself gently supported from both sides.

"Good night, Your Majesty." He yawned with heavy eyelids. "I'm . . . I'm sorry to have faded so soon. Please forgive me."

"Never mind that," said the king. "Sleep as late as you want. I'll wait to hear from you, and hope we are able to continue with this extraordinary recitation."

"Oh, I'll be all right by tomorrow, Your Majesty." Bidpai perked up. "Don't worry. Good night, Sire, and sleep well."

"Good night, Dr. Bidpai," said the king.

The next afternoon Bidpai was as good as his word.

"I feel tremendously refreshed," he said to Dabschelim, once they were seated in the observatory. "I believe the second of Houschenk's precepts goes: 'Always preserve your ministers, counsellors, and grandees in a balance of mutual understanding with one another, that they may unanimously labour for the good of the state.'"

"Yes, yes, that's correct," said Dabschelim as he peered at Farsi's translation of the treasure document.

"Well, this precept is illustrated in the story of 'Zirac and Friends,'" said Bidpai, "otherwise known as 'How to Win Friends.' It goes like this.

*I have
never found
an orientalist
who could deny
that a single
shelf of a
good European
library
was worth
the whole
native
literature
of India
and Arabia.*

Macaulay

*Grief knits
two hearts in
closer bonds
than happiness
ever can; and
common suffer-
ings are far
stronger links
than common
joys.*

Lamartine

ZIRAC AND FRIENDS

A certain old and knowing crow once nested in a mighty sambal tree that rose up high into the sky from the edge of an ancient forest. Her young were long since grown and flown, and life seemed an endless pause of peace until that morning when she saw a hunter creeping from tree to tree towards her home. Every feathered friend in the area grew quiet as a motionless stone. Not a peep escaped while hundreds of glinting birds' eyes peered at the man's sneaky movements. Off his shoulders he lifted a loop of netting and carefully unrolled it near the foot of friend crow's tree. He scattered a pocketful of yellow corn through the mesh, then tiptoed off into some bushes not too far away and waited.

'Alarm! Alarm!' vigorously cawed our heroine. 'Beware the nets! Beware the nets! Hunter! Hunter!'

Every other bird in the neighbourhood also sang out a warning tune, and soon a great surge of tweets, whistles, whoops, twitters, screeches, chirrups, honks, hoots, squawks, clucks, and peep-peep-peeps lifted

185

towards the skies. Yet even this cacophonous mix of apprehensive cries failed to alert a flock of pigeons cruising overhead. Either they were too high or their beating wings drowned all extra sound.

In any case, their leader, King Sharpeyes, suddenly glimpsed the tiniest yellow gleam of possibly beautiful corn, and rolled left to begin a great swooping dive earthward. A couple of hundred pigeons followed immediately behind him, spread out like a magically flickering fan which shifted elegantly open, turned, spun, and contracted as the flock spiralled downward. The whoosh of wind in their descent excluded all warnings from those anxious birds below, and when the pigeons landed at the base of crow's tree, intent on gobbling up the now highly alluring corn, a great many of their feet were immediately snared in the hidden net.

For a moment there was complete panic. The trapped pigeons fluttered about, pulling their feet tighter and tighter into the filament of the netting or uselessly pecking at the entanglements with their beaks. With a sudden squawk of horror, King Sharpeyes perceived the extent of his error and froze on the spot.

'Listen,' he shouted in a firm pigeon-leader's voice. 'Everyone stop moving in isolation. Keep still. My mistake about this corn will end in disaster unless we co-ordinate our efforts. We must concentrate our energies, not scatter them.'

There was a lull throughout the flock as everyone quieted down.

'Quickly now!' he continued. 'Mischief is close at wing. We must escape or perish. All together, then. When I count three, flap for your life. We're going to steal this cursed net rather than let it snatch down our hopes. Ready? *One . . . Two . . .*'

'*Eeeyyaaah!*' screamed the fowler as he burst out of hiding from behind the bushes and charged the flock, brandishing a cudgel overhead, intent on mayhem.

'*Three!*' shouted Sharpeyes, and in that instant every snared member of the flock gave the best flaps of its life. Those few pigeons who had been lucky enough to avoid the net now pitched in, and, using beak or claws, grabbed a strand here or there and flew for all they were worth.

Believe it or not, the pigeons succeeded. The net was plucked neatly and suddenly from the ground and rose irregularly in the air, hovering like a darkish cloud of droopy lace. The fowler froze in his tracks and dropped his club. His mouth hung open like an idiot's as he watched those that were getting away.

'Come on, you cooers!' yelled Sharpeyes. 'Put your backs into it. Unite your wings and fly! Onward and upward!'

The flock bestirred itself to strive with even greater effort, and soon, with wings beating more fiercely than ever, the pigeons found their collective rhythm and the whole aerial conglomeration of net and bird abandoned the edge of the forest and took off across the fields.

'Higher!' exhorted Sharpeyes. 'We must gain more altitude!' And sure enough, in only a little while, they achieved exactly that. Meanwhile the hunter, suddenly released from the statuehood of his stupefaction, picked up his cudgel and ran after his flying net.

'Such unheard-of teamwork cannot last long,' he grumbled darkly to himself. 'Soon they must come to roost, so if I follow quickly I'll still eat pigeon pie.'

And what of gallant crow, our friend perched way up in the sambal tree? She could scarce believe what both her eyes had seen. She had to know more, to find out how the matter ended. Impelled by delightful quiverings of curiosity, she launched forth and flew past the scrambling fowler until she caught up with that handsome Sharpeyes and his flapping crew.

'Old two-legs is following,' Sharpeyes was shouting, 'hoping we will tire. We must lose him for good by flying over more rugged terrain.' He caught his breath, for it was a great exertion to fly in these conditions and command at the same time.

'Heave-ho, me hearties,' he continued. 'Swing to our right and head towards those wooded hills. He'll despair in the brambles and thickets, and if our luck holds we'll reach the home of my friend, Zirac the rat.'

King Sharpeyes broke into a fit of coughing and sputtering as flock and net wheeled round in the sky and set off in the new direction. 'Damn your tiredness,' he shouted louder than ever between his gasps and retches, 'and flap with all you've got.'

Considering the steady drag of the net, the flock did remarkably well. It was quite extraordinary to watch this peculiar flying object climbing over hill and dale, and soon the fowler was being left farther behind. He cursed and stumbled on, working himself into a rage of frustration as the steepness of the ground increased. Finally he stopped, stamping his feet in fury. It was obvious that the trees which now towered in front of him would soon screen the pigeons from view, and the thickness of the underbrush was slowing him down more and more.

'You net thieves!' he shouted, shaking his fist after the vanishing gauze in the sky. 'You evil birds, depriving an honest man of his tools!' And, his anger vented, the fowler shrugged and stomped off back towards home.

Sharpeyes noticed this retreat only seconds before the treetops began to obscure the distant fowler. 'We've done it!' he shouted in a voice beginning to crack with strain. 'He's given up!'

The pigeons and their dangling net flew on for another few miles until they passed over the deserted ruins of an ancient castle. A few walls and battlements—one topped with an intact turret—remained standing in isolated disarray, covered by great green tangles of vine and creeper. The extent and size of the place indicated that it had once teemed with men, but that was now long, long ago.

'Down there, over by that mound,' called out Sharpeyes. 'Zirac lives at the bottom. Land! Land!' The exhausted pigeons eased off on their flap rate and aimed themselves and the net down to the indicated spot. The mound was bald and rocky, and looked like the roof of some underground chamber. Meanwhile, old crow headed for a tree that overlooked the scene, and perched there preening her feathers, keeping an eye on all that happened.

The net dragged across the ground before collapsing in a series of moving folds. Next the pigeons tumbled in and lay in a scattered heap of sprawling bodies, more tired than words can tell. Their little pounding hearts seemed about to pop from their throats like warm, vibrant plums, and many felt they would surely die from their exertions.

Such was not to be. The collective gasps, wheezes, groans, coughs, sighs, splutters, and choking sounds which arose from the flopped flock gradually tailed off into uniform deep breathings. King Sharpeyes recovered sufficiently to call out:

'Zirac! Zirac, my friend! Where are you?'

Now Zirac was nothing if not a cautious rat. As a safeguard against sudden attacks from any direction, he had constructed dozens of strategically placed entrance and exit holes in his burrow. And although he had not seen the pigeons landing with their net, the fluttering of their wings had been loud and strange enough to wake him from a doze and send him instinctively scurrying deep within the recesses of his home. When he heard his own name being called, he was, to be sure, startled, and crept towards the light of a certain entrance hole very carefully indeed.

'Zirac here,' he answered loudly from inside. 'Who's calling?'

'Why, it's King Sharpeyes, your old friend—Big Pige, the pigeon. Come quickly, please. We're in terrible trouble and need your help.'

Zirac poked just his nose out, sniffing the air furiously and blinking like mad in the daylight.

'Good God, bird!' he exclaimed when his eyes had adjusted sufficiently to survey the scene. 'However did you get yourself into this mess?' For a moment the rat stood transfixed as he peered at the amazing prospect of a couple of hundred panting, snared pigeons on his doorstep.

'Well,' said Sharpeyes, 'it's the usual story of faulty perception and fantastic expectation. My own, I'm afraid, in this case. I saw the corn but not the net: looked with my stomach, got snatched by the feet. Such is the beauty and the beast of all selective vision and the principle of every trap. We were lucky that our trap was light and we still had wings to fly. And so we did, and it was hard—believe me, friend—to flee the fowler, and now you see us helpless here, dependent on your kindness and the sharpness of your teeth.'

'What a pretty speech, my bird!' laughed Zirac, scampering down the side of the mound towards Sharpeyes. 'At least you've remained cheerful during your little escapade.'

The rat came close to his friend, squatted back on his haunches and stretched upward, wrinkling his nose as he inspected the situation. Because the net had caught a wing in landing, Sharpeyes's head was now trussed up next to his shoulder at such an awkward angle that he could scarcely move. Zirac shook

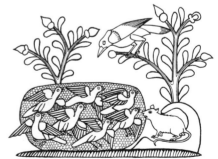

his head slowly from side to side in mock disbelief and gave a high-pitched snort that was gruffer than a squeak.

'Not too comfortable, then, are we?' he asked in that teasing tone reserved for special mates. 'Well, never mind, Sharpeyes, old feather-face. I'll set you right in a jiffy.'

With that he began nipping and snipping at the meshes of the net with his gleaming, gnashing incisors. They were very sharp, for one or two precise chomps followed by a little gnaw usually sufficed to sever each strand, and Zirac worked so fast that his teeth clattered softly like some efficient miniature machine.

'Hold it! Hold it!' said Sharpeyes. 'Leave me and do the others first. Zirac! Do you hear me? Please!'

The rat ignored the pigeon and continued rattling away at his job. Sharpeyes repeated his request. Zirac stopped and pulled back.

'Listen, pal,' he said. 'What's the matter? Do you want to stay like that? What if a hawk should fly past and spot you? Or a man walk by? Those archaeologist types sometimes come snooping around here. Now just shut up and let me get on with it.'

'No,' said Sharpeyes. 'Attend to the others first. Free them before me.'

'Are you crazy?' said the rat. 'You don't want to get free as soon as possible? What's the matter with you? You're the *leader*, not some nobody. Besides, you're the one who's my friend—not them!'

'That's exactly my point,' said Sharpeyes. 'Although I dropped them in this mess, they pulled me out. Such allegiance puts me in their debt. Their safety comes before my little life, which undeserves their love.'

'Great balls of furry mice!' exclaimed Zirac. 'Whatever are you talking about, you silly bird?'

'Look here, Zirac—noble rat and long-time friend— my idea is simply practical. If you free me first, you might tire before you release the rest. But if I am last, I know you'll never leave me. Relieve the others of their pain and fear while waiting, thus, to free me from my own.'

'By God, you're a winner!' exclaimed Zirac. 'I love you, you insane feather-duster,' he said, and he stretched his head forward to give the snared pigeon a clumsy but very affectionate forehead biff, a neck nuzzle, and maybe even a kiss. 'Okay, then, Crazy-beak,' he said. 'Here goes.'

Zirac began to sever the meshes in which all the rest were bound. He lost count after he had freed a hundred and fifty pigeons. In the end it cost him over five solid hours of teeth-numbing gnaws before he encountered Sharpeyes again who, once freed, and after rolling his head around on his neck a few times to relieve some very cramped muscles, gave thanks as follows:

'Good rat, what is there we can say? Our lives are yours. For us the Zirac years now begin. This bonus to our time will flower in our hearts, and wherever we may fly, memory will hoist aloft the special features of your face and the shining emblem of your deed. With us this tale will never die, of that you may be sure.'

'Aw, cut the flattery,' said Zirac. 'You want my ears to burst into flame? Come on—get out of here and leave

me alone. It's siesta time and my teeth are tired. See
you around, feather-face. See you around.'

With that he made his way back through the flock
which was gathered well to one side of the demolished
net.

'Hip hip, hooray!' someone cooed from within the
crowd. 'Long live Zirac, the razor-toothed rat!' Immediately great soft pigeon cheers filled the air as all paid
tribute to their rodent rescuer, and Zirac, though he
pretended to be concerned only with stretching his
aching jaws by wriggling his lips and opening and
closing his mouth, nevertheless felt pleasantly soothed
by the gentle murmuration of their cooings—not to
mention the frequent brush of feathers against his fur
as he scuttled towards his nearest hole. Reaching it, he
turned quickly, leaned back on his haunches, and
rather sheepishly acknowledged the adoring bird
throng with a half-smile and three or four brief, one-
pawed waves, rolled his eyes, and in a flash was gone
deep into his burrow. After a few minutes the commotion of delightful thanksgiving settled down as the
flock set about its business.

King Sharpeyes made a quick speech of abdication,
saying that, because of his faulty perception, he must
remove himself from power. But this move was most
vigorously cooed down amid a great ruffling of feathers
and clacking of beaks. Then the eldest and wisest pigeon of them all captured every heart when he strutted
somewhat dodderingly forward to exclaim:

'Whatever error you committed, O King, by leading
us *into* the net, you cancelled by leading us off *with* the

net. Events spiral back to where they were, and you must certainly remain The King!'

And so it was. Sharpeyes's bid to withdraw from power was unanimously rejected. He accepted this graciously, his eyes lowered to the ground while the pigeon-cheering burst out around him.

'*Sharp . . . eyes . . . Sharp . . . eyes . . .* Long live King Sharp . . . eyes!'

And when this excitement had eventually calmed down and he knew every eye was on him, Sharpeyes suddenly looked up and beamed his attention into the receptive flock as his head scanned first left then right.

'Right, then,' he said softly, and everyone strained forward to catch his every word. 'What about some food? There's nothing here except rock and ruin. But I'm pretty sure I spotted a field of young wheat on our flightpath here. And I'm equally sure there was no net, but of course we'll check it out very carefully before landing. So what do we say? Are we hungry?'

Of course they were, and in less time than it takes to tell, our friend crow was watching the pigeons wheeling off into the skyway against the evening sun. A great quiet descended over the place, and as crow peered about from her perch in the tree, she felt just a little bit lonely. It didn't really matter, though, for she had already decided to spend the night. You see, she knew Zirac was there, sleeping away in his burrow somewhere, and that fact made any hardship possible for, believe it or not, she had fallen in love with this razor-toothed rat.

Bright and early the next morning, after only a short

worm or two for breakfast, crow hops up to one of rat's holes and begins calling down it very sweetly in a singsong voice:

'Zirac . . . O Zirac . . . Come out and see me, please.'

'Who's making all that racket at this time of day?' Zirac yells back. 'Go away and leave me alone.'

'There's a crow named Shesheen here, hoping to be your friend. Come and see. Come and see. Zirac . . . O Zirac . . .'

'Oh, shut up and get out of here! A crow? Don't be ridiculous. We can't be friends: we're born enemies, you and I. Now flap off!'

'Oh, how can you be so cruel, you rat?' Shesheen caws softly down the hole in a tearful voice. 'Just suppose for a second that I am sincere: what then of your quick assumption?'

Now this plea quite touches Zirac and, his curiosity aroused, he scurries partway up this particular hole to get a better—though entirely safe—look at the crow. All he can see through his opening is a wrinkled pair of crow's feet.

'Hey, out there,' he shouts. 'Move back a bit so I can see your beak when you're talking. What's all this rubbish, then? Exactly why do you want to be my friend? What's your motive?'

Shesheen springs back twice and cocks her head over to try and catch a glimpse of her hero in his hole, but it isn't much use. Peer intently as she may, all she can perceive in the narrow obscurity is perhaps the barest hint of a beady rat eye or two.

'O Wonderful One,' she says in a very pleasant voice,

'when I witnessed what you did for Sharpeyes and the others, my heart trembled and my feathers quivered. Never before has selfless brotherhood so twanged my nerve wires: all my attention sped to that noble deed. I felt I could not bear a life of separation from such a source of safety and delight. What if calamity ever netted me? Where would be a Zirac to ensure my release? I felt alone, merely a bird among birds, and knew the need of diversity: my wings and your teeth, for example. Each creature has its speciality, and it is to redeem my incompleteness that I come, hoping my reliability may mutually serve your own, and our new friendship bring greater ease to each. Please do not say no to this most heartfelt of all requests.'

'Hey, hey, Babble-beak—what's with all the words?' Zirac calls out after only the briefest pause. 'What are you trying to do? Blind me with theory? Avalanche me with flattery? So you want to be my friend: this is wonderful news! Now get out of here. You're a crow and I'm a rat. Do we try to climb a waterfall or swim a tree just because we feel like it? What can't be done can't be done.'

He pauses for a moment and scurries a bit closer to the light so that the crow now catches a better view of his ratty features. His whiskers twitch earnestly as he stretches to snuffle briefly at the bird.

'Look, Shesheen,' he says, 'this is impossible. You're bigger than I am. One stab from your beak and I'm dead. How can we be friends if whenever you get hungry I'm suddenly your food? So go rook someone else, Gobble-guts—okay?'

'And who would want to eat you, you little useless
bag of fur!' Shesheen clacks back. 'Do you think I can't
find a better snack elsewhere? That I have to spend my
time trying to outwit some scrawny ratmeat? You're
suffering from delusions of delectability! Since when
do crows specialize in rats anyway? I've never been a
rat-pecker, and don't intend to start now. What do you
think I am, a feathered cat?'

'Okay, okay,' answers Zirac, slightly annoyed at
being caught out in the seeming irrationality of his
fear. 'But say what you like, I'm not budging from this
hole. Kindness cannot disguise our inequalities. You
can hurt me more than I can hurt you. Whatever con-
geniality we might muster, crisis would point to our
differences—much as boiling water douses a fire if the
vessel of shared heat tips over.'

'Oooou . . . eeee! Well said, O Rat, and you do have a
point! Clever clever! Never mind, though; I am still determined to outface your lack of trust. You have risk in
littleness, yes—but my real intent brings safety. I truly
prize your goodness, and would alloy your mettle with
my own to make a substance doubly strong. Thus
friendship could, if it were born, become our greatest
strength. But listen, now: enough of words. I'm staying
here on hunger strike until I starve or you come out!'

'Starve away then, starve away,' says Zirac. 'It may
be that you *are* good and intend me no harm, but good
cannot come of such a friendship. Nature will assert
itself in the end; the love of horse and ass dies finally
with the mule. A man can charm a cobra with his
music pipe, but only a fool sleeps with such a snake.'

'I don't want to sleep with you, you rat! I just want to be around you, near you, talk with you, learn about you. Listen: I'm a respecter of privacy and I hope you are too! I live in trees and you live in the ground—so what's your worry? Just come out of your hole so I can see you again. Stop all this arguing and let's make peace. What's the matter? I want to be your friend!'

'Okay, okay,' says Zirac. 'I'm coming. I give up; you win. I was only testing, you know. I had to be sure there was at least a chance of honesty from you.'

The rat runs to the opening of his hole, sticks out his head and smiles crookedly at Shesheen, who is standing quietly back.

'Even now,' he says, 'you could be conning me, but never mind. I've decided to trust you, come what may. We both know you can win any fight between us, so what the hell. If you are lying, at least you'll remember you didn't win me over through cleverness. No, my friend—it's my decision to trust you, and I accept full responsibility for this exposure of my vulnerability.'

'Then why are you hesitating in the entrance of your hole?' Shesheen asks softly. 'Why don't you come all the way out? Are you frightened?'

The rat stares straight into the crow's dark eyes for a long moment.

'Yes,' he says, 'I am frightened. My entire body resists the unnatural desire to approach danger. It comprehends flight or fight, but friendship and trust with someone more powerful—that's a different story. In short, my body thinks my decision is crazy.'

'Do you still distrust me?' asks the crow.

'I don't know,' says Zirac. 'In the assessment of reliability, speech never substitutes for behaviour. To be frank, all I have from you so far is a bunch of wonderful words plus some rather insignificant actions. Do they mean anything? Only time will tell. There are two types of friend: the friend of the heart and the friend of the eye. The faces of both smile, but with different intent. The difference between them is expectation; one looks for something, the other doesn't. Bait never dangles from a hook to benefit the belly of a fish!'

'All right, all right,' says Shesheen impatiently, 'but what has this to do with me? Why are you still afraid?'

'Look,' says Zirac, 'I accept that you and I may well learn to trust each other. But what about your friends? What if another crow appears who knows nothing of us and, say, acting hastily, goes for my eyes? Tries to eat me?'

'Oh, stop it!' exclaims Shesheen. 'You're being absurd. If you're my friend, I'm going to protect you. Any enemy of yours is an enemy of mine. Anyway, I'm a widow and don't have many friends—crow or otherwise—so stop dreaming up irrational fears.'

'You're right!' says Zirac. 'I give in totally now! Here I come, you gleamy-eyed bird-bag.' And he rushes out and madly embraces the crow.

Naturally Shesheen is overcome with delight and returns Zirac's vigorous advances. After much kissing and joy, their enthusiasm gradually calms down and things enter a more practical

phase. They don't exactly set up house together—
that's impossible. Let's say, however, that they coordi-
nate habitats.

In accordance with needs, each went the way of its
own species, but once these basic differences were satisfied, they spent a great deal of time together. In the
weeks that followed, they had long and earnest dis-
cussions about every topic under the sun and moon.
Hardly a day passed without Shesheen flying in some
dainty morsel of meat, beakful of grain, or insect for
Zirac to eat, and the rat likewise was constantly be-
stowing upon this enraptured lady crow not only his
choice of special tidbits but also, from time to time,
jewelled trinkets and other shiny gewgaws that he had
rummaged from somewhere under the castle ruins.

Shesheen could spend hours gazing at these testa-
ments to Zirac's devotion, her head cocked over as she
cast her gimlet eyes beyond the tip of her beak and
deep into the hypnotic mystery of glitter-glitter. She
hid these special treasures in the crook of a favourite
tree, and flew them down one by one and placed them
on the ground on those days when she felt a need for
diversion; a guided dream, as it were, towards memory's endless kiss of being beautiful forever and desir-
able always. Zirac carefully kept his distance during
these private moments.

This was a happy time when the plains of contentment surrounded both their lives. Each creature
always looked back upon that stretch of peace as their
honeymoon of friendship, but, as is the way with everyone, eventually novelty wore thin and subtle

changes began to shift from somewhere deep within.

It was Zirac who displayed the symptoms first. He gradually became quieter and more withdrawn. An untypical edge of cynicism slipped into his humour. To put it bluntly, he soon turned into a very sour rat indeed.

'What's the matter?' Shesheen asked gently one day when Zirac sat enveloped in gloom, listlessly pawing over some food she had just given him. 'You've been looking very depressed lately.'

'Have I?' said the rat. 'Oh, I see. Well, not to worry. I've just been feeling a bit thoughtful. That's all.'

'And what have you been thinking about?'

'Oh, nothing much. The usual things. Time. Life. Death. You know. Stuff like that.'

'I see,' said the crow, and she turned and hopped away a short distance. 'And have you come to any practical conclusions?' she threw over her shoulder without glancing back.

Zirac looked up sharply. 'Practical conclusions?' he snorted indignantly. 'Practical conclusions! No, certainly not. Why do you ask?'

'Well,' said the crow, turning round again, 'I don't mind admitting I'm a bit worried about you. I don't wish to interfere, but you've definitely not been your usual cheery self of late. Maybe it's time you tried to wrap it up.'

'Wrap it up!' bristled the rat. 'Wrap what up? What are you talking about?'

'Well, you know,' said Shesheen, 'this morbid thinking. I mean, is it getting you anywhere?'

'How should I know?' snapped Zirac. 'Look! Why can't you just leave me alone? Let's just say I'm fed up with this place, okay? I'll get through this irritable patch, don't you worry. Just leave me in peace for a while, and give things a chance to sort themselves out.'

'Certainly, certainly,' said Shesheen, 'but please— tell me briefly what it is about this place that upsets you. I ask only because I've felt something similar myself lately, and wonder if we are both sharing the same experience.'

'Same experience, my whiskers!' exclaimed Zirac. 'I've never really liked this place since I came here. Now what's your excuse?'

'But I thought you were born around here,' said Shesheen.

'No,' said the rat. 'I originally came from the city. I'm not a country rat at all.'

'That's interesting. What brought you here?'

'That's a long story for another time and another place. I promise to tell it to you someday—but not now! So if you don't mind . . .'

'Why don't we move away?' asked Shesheen. 'Nothing is stopping us.'

'*What?*' asked Zirac incredulously.

'It's not exactly as if we have a lot to carry, is it?' continued the crow.

'Where would we go?' asked the rat. 'What do you think we are—a couple of characters who can simply turn up and check into the nearest hotel?'

'I know a place,' said Shesheen. 'I have a friend, a turtle named Slowpoke, and—'

'Slowpoke the turtle! I see . . . uh-huh. Sure . . . sure.
And ole Slowpoke runs a nice little country inn
where—'

'No, it's not like that at all! He lives in an isolated
pond full of cool, clear water and plenty of fish which
he catches and feeds to his guests. I'm telling you, I've
been there and it's great. What do you say?'

'All right, let's go.'

'You mean it?'

'Yeah, why not? What have I got to lose? Let's go.'

'All right. Stick up your tail.'

'Stick up my tail?'

'Yes. You don't think we're going to walk, do you?'

'No . . . no . . . but . . .'

'Well, stick up your tail!'

'Oh, all right, you dratted bird!' said Zirac, and he
turned around and shot his tail straight up into the air,
stiff as a stick. 'Come on, then, Lady Fleetwing,' he
muttered with his snout practically in the dust. 'Let's
get this show into the sky. Here we come, Mr. Slowpoke—ready or not!'

'Lower your tail over towards your right,' Shesheen
called out. 'About forty-five degrees, but keep it
straight.' She skipped backwards enough distance to
give herself a good run-in, and although Zirac grumbled incoherently to himself, he did as she asked.

'Fine,' said the crow. 'That's great. Hold it there.'
Then she extended her wings and began a flapping,
hopping scramble towards Zirac with her beak wide
open and her head tilted over to the left. Her feet had
just cleared the ground and she was hurtling along

when Zirac's stiff tail slotted neatly into the vee of her beak. Tightly but not too tightly, she locked onto the rat's tail, levelled her head, put on full lift with a rapid series of mighty, spiralling flaps, and snatched him straight up into the air.

'Owwwwww!' yelled the rat as he dangled dizzyingly downward. 'Did you have to jerk me up so hard? Who issued you your pilot's licence? Never mind. Don't answer any questions. Just keep quiet and concentrate on the flying.' And to contribute what little he could to his own safety, Zirac snaked the loose end of his tail a couple of times around Shesheen's beak.

They travelled together in this peculiar manner for twenty or thirty minutes, but to the rat it seemed a breathless eternity through most of which he kept his eyes tightly shut. Each time he dared peek out upon the open world below, terror smartly squeezed his eyelids down. By the end of the journey, however, he had grown so accustomed to the vast horizon spread beneath his blood-rushed head that he could relax with open eyes.

'Why, it's beautiful!' he finally burst out as Shesheen began her descent towards Slowpoke's abode. 'What a world you birds behold from up here! Us landlubbers simply have no idea of what you see! Oh, I hope you'll take me up again someday. I think I rather like it, no matter what an ache it gives my tail.'

They soared down over Slowpoke's pond, a spring-fed body of dark water that shimmered placidly from a gentle hollow in the landscape. From the air it indeed appeared to be an inviting little place, isolated within a verdant sweep of grasslands and remote from the habitations of men. A few dozen pleasant trees were clumped together in a shady copse on the north shore, and peace and stillness seemed the order of the day.

Slowpoke lay sunning himself on a log that stuck half in and half out of the water. His shell was a mottled greenish-brown and blended perfectly with the background. You wouldn't have spotted him from the air unless you'd been looking very carefully, and then you would certainly have remarked what a large, handsome turtle he was.

Shesheen and the dangling Zirac swooped down low and whizzed across the water towards Slowpoke. One of the turtle's eyes snapped wide open and registered the approach of this airborne apparition.

'Hello there!' Zirac sang out happily as they buzzed by. 'Lovely day!'

With a great smack, Slowpoke threw himself into the water and vanished from sight.

Shesheen glided across the pond and swept up into a braking position, flaps down, hovering furiously with all her strength as she gently lowered Zirac among some smooth rocks by the bank. Touching down, the rat unwound his tail from Shesheen's beak and scuttled away into a natural hidey-hole in the rocks. He whirled about and faced the fresh scene before him with a huge, eager grin.

Shesheen had landed and was busy ruffling her feathers, craning her neck, and generally shaking her body about to relieve the muscular stresses, strains, and stiffnesses which were brief legacies from her first ratty passenger trip. However, as soon as she had caught her breath and preened herself to readiness, she began calling out over the water to the missing turtle:

'Slowpoke, you big monster! Come on up. It's Shesheen, your old friend. Hey, Slowpoke, don't be shy.'

It was some time before the turtle heard these earnest pleas. He didn't poke his head above water until he was safely hidden among the reeds along the opposite shore. And even then he proceeded very cautiously, without making a single bubble or even the slightest swirl, sticking first only his nose, next his eyes, and finally his earholes above the surface. He squinted through the reed stalks in the crow's direction and listened intently to her voice.

'Ahoy, there, Queen Shesheen!' he finally announced in a deep gravelly voice that boomed across the pond. 'It sounds like you now, but it certainly didn't a moment ago. What's happened to your face?'

'There's two of us, Slowpoke, two of us,' Shesheen called back. 'Myself and Zirac the rat. We've come for a visit if it's convenient.'

'Ho ho,' called the turtle. 'Hang on a minute. I'll be right with you.' He sank down among the reeds and a moment or two later his head popped up in the middle of the pond.

'Well well well,' he rumbled as he swam towards his visitors. 'Long time no see, Shesheen. Long time no see.' Soon he was wading and splashing ashore, and the crow hopped forward to greet him with open wings.

'Hello, you sassy old Witchbird,' Slowpoke said as they exchanged affectionate pecks, nips, and nudges. 'What do you mean "if it's convenient?" Who else does a retired sailor get to talk to aside from his friends? Why, shiver my bodyshell, of course it's convenient! Yo ho ho and a pond full of fish! Ha!'

With an ominous glare and his jaw jutting out pugnaciously, he plodded bowleggedly up to the rocks, looking so relentlessly formidable that Shesheen retreated before him with little bounces and springs.

'Quawk! Queewk! Queewk!' screeched the crow. 'Stop it! Stop it, you brute! What are you doing?'

The turtle totally ignored the flapping bird, pushed by her, and with a sudden and quite amazing smile in contrast to his earlier demeanour, opened his eyes twinklingly wide and addressed himself to the rocks.

'Welcome aboard Black Pond, Mr. Zirac,' he said, 'if that's you I see smiling away there in the background. I suppose it's some kind of recommendation if you've appeared under the wings of this demented aviatrix. Ha!'

'Zirac, just call me Zirac,' said the rat, as he scampered out into the afternoon sunlight to greet the big turtle with lots of delighted little nods and smiles. 'Thank you, captain,' he said. 'Thank you for having me.'

'Ho ho!' said the turtle. 'Don't mention it. We'll have a grand time, don't you worry. Now, how about something to eat? I'm going fishing soon, but in the meantime maybe you'd like a little snack. Can I . . . er . . .

interest you perhaps in a few easily gathered *escargots
au nature?* You know, snails . . . gastropods, slowly
slithering members of the family Mollusca. We turtles
love them very much, and the other end of the pond pro-
duces a superb variety. Or maybe you'd prefer a nice
serving of slimy slugs. We have them as well, though
a bit farther inland. Speak, Zirac. What will it be?'

'Whatever's easiest,' replied the rat. 'I don't mind.
Anything will do.'

'Shesheen, what about you?' asked the turtle over
his carapace. 'I assume you'll join us.'

'Have you any turtle soup?' teased the crow.

'Ha!' exclaimed Slowpoke, and he began turning
slowly around, grinding the sand and stones trapped
beneath his plastron. 'Ha!' he exclaimed again, when
he eventually faced the crow.

'Come along, Lady Pinfeathers,' he menaced gruffly.
'We'll leave Zirac to make himself at home while you
and I get some chow ready. I'll hunt for it and you can
be the pretty waitress. Heh heh! . . . Zirac!' he cried.

'Yes, captain!' answered the rat, as he quickly ran
around to the turtle's head. 'What is it?'

'Just a suggestion. You might find it a bit more comfortable to set up camp under that third tree on your
right over there.' The turtle lifted up a front leg and
awkwardly pointed in the direction indicated with a
hooked foreclaw. 'There's lots of exposed roots, old
leaves, and tufts of grass around its base—plenty for
you to dig yourself into, in other words. You'll be staying a few nights, I assume?'

'Well, yes, of course we will, if that's an invitation.'

'Ha! Of course it is, you silly wee beastie!'

'Well, thank you very much, captain. Thank you very much indeed.'

'Never mind that,' said Slowpoke. 'I'll see you later with some fish if my luck's any good. In the meantime Shesheen here can fly back the hors d'oeuvres. Now you just make yourself at home, Zirac, and take it easy. 'Bye for now.'

'Goodbye,' said the rat.

'See you soon,' said Shesheen, and she hopped onto Slowpoke's back for a free yet lumbering ride down to the water's edge.

And so it was that the three friends began a very enjoyable evening. Zirac soon scooped out a warm and dry little burrow under the tree indicated by Slowpoke, and settled himself very comfortably indeed. Shesheen flew in with several choice beakfuls of slugs and snails which both she and the rat agreed were the most absolutely scrumptious appetizers they'd ever tasted in their lives. Later, but not much later, Slowpoke suddenly broke the pond's surface with a frantic carp gripped tightly between his crushing jaws. He swam ashore, and together he and Shesheen quickly killed the fish before dragging it under Zirac's tree. Then the feasting truly began. As they consumed the delicious flesh of the carp, the three animals talked and joked among themselves in such a way that each felt enriched and none neglected. It soon became apparent, much to Shesheen's delight, that Slowpoke and Zirac, after a certain initial wariness, were veering towards genuine fondness. The deep laughter of the turtle rumbled across the pond when Shesheen delighted him with the story of how Sharpeyes and his flock escaped the fowler. The crow also recounted, naturally enough, her first sight of Zirac rescuing snared pigeons from a net; and the rat answered this by describing his own tail-twirling experience of bird flight that very day. And so time passed pleasantly in the warmth of good company until the evening sun nestled down below the red-streaked cloud bellies that trooped across the sky in solid crimson force. Over the three friends loomed twilight's eerie hush, and quietly they paused in its stillness, turning their heads westward to watch the fade of day. Shesheen flapped up to a nearby branch for a better view. It was a long while before Zirac spoke, and when he did it was dark.

'Thank you,' he said, 'thank you both for having me. Your hospitality, Slowpoke, is unsurpassed; and, Shesheen, you were very clever to fly me here today. I feel a very different and significantly improved rat over what I was this morning. And to express my gratitude, if you're both interested, I would like to tell the full story of how I came to live alone in the ruins of the castle where Shesheen first met me. She asked me about my past, in fact, only this morning, so I know she's curious. But how about you, Slowpoke? I don't want to bore you.'

'Stop dillydallying and get on with it,' said the turtle amicably.

'Right,' said Zirac. 'Settle yourselves comfortably, then. Here we go.'

Super Rat and the Monks

'I was born and raised in the town of Mahila, and after I left the home of my parents, I went to live in a monastery on the outskirts. I stayed in the cell of a monk named Charlie, and for several years led a very pleasant existence.

Every morning Charlie would venture into town with his begging bowl and scrounge the necessary food to keep himself alive. However, as he knew and hated, it wasn't only himself he fed, but me as well. In fact so good were the pickings at Charlie's place that word got around, and soon I was feeding a whole crowd of other rats as well. I didn't mind; they were friends, or at least so I thought, and there was plenty for everyone.

Charlie would return every day around noon, sit at his table and eat maybe half his beggings while keeping a wary eye out for me and, when he was finished, put away the leftovers for his evening meal, hanging his begging bowl by its neck chain on a nail high in the wall. But these precautions never did him much good because I always found a way to reach his begging bowl while he was out.

After lunch Charlie would go off to do whatever it is monks are supposed to do with their afternoons: study, meditate, work in the communal gardens—something like that, I'm not really sure what. In any case his departure was the signal for me to begin. No matter where Charlie hung his begging bowl or how he tried to cover it up, I always managed to get to it. I was a prodigious jumper in those days—fearless, it seemed, of any risk of missing or falling. My friends

would gather round underneath and cheer me on with stirring grunts and squeaks as I clambered onto the table or along a shelf to launch myself towards the food hoard. I even had a route for reaching the rafters of the room so I could leap downward in case Charlie got clever, stood on a chair, and hung his begging bowl extra high off the floor.

Nothing he tried ever did him any good. He set traps, left poison, shifted his begging from morning to evening, but even while he slept nearby I managed to get my paws into his food. I would eat my fill and throw out the rest to my companions. They, in turn, showered me with exciting attention.

"Good old Zirac," the males would say. "What a champ. Here, I've brought you something I found in the garden. Wow—what a jump that was you made last night!"

The lady rats would send me eye-messages, making it very clear that it wasn't just food they thought I might be good for. "Hey, fella," one of them once whispered when I hadn't quite woken to the situation, "why don't you try jumping on me sometime?" And with a flash of her tail she shot off, leaving me momentarily dumbfounded until my whiskers perked up and I bounded after her (she'd been sweet enough to pause and glance back so as not to get *too* far ahead!).

Oh, it was grand while it lasted, all right. We called ourselves Charlie's Devils in mockery of our meek, unwilling keeper, and I, simply because of my jumping ability, discovered the giddy delights of power—never realizing for a moment on what a feeble foundation my role rested. In fact, it never occurred to me that things might not go on like this forever. But I found out soon enough from that day when Charlie's friend arrived.

My life in this period remains like a happy dream from childhood; I have no idea how long it burgeoned. For years I seemed unfailingly accurate, confounding the odds and always reaching my objective. Certainly, part of my success stemmed from the feebleness of Charlie's character. He was not a forceful individual, but tall and thin with a stoop of the shoulders that curved his posture into the shape of a question mark. He had constantly rheumy eyes and a sniffly nose that always seemed to be dribbling. His voice, when he spoke, was high and irregularly squeaky, like chalk screeching along a blackboard. He was, in short, a phenomenon of reverse charisma; Charlie positively radiated gloom, sucking in joy from all around him and rendering the atmosphere leaden and dingy. How he ever managed to succeed as a beggar, I never knew. Perhaps people pitied him for his inordinate number of unfortunate traits.

In any case, Charlie's friend, by contrast, seemed an exclamation point of gusto! He crackled with interest in the world about him, his mind drawn by natural curiosity towards the reconciliation of detail. If anything, his prying nature came on a trifle overbearing and he was, indeed, a stout, bald, bullish man—thickset and pushy with energy. He shoved his way into situations, insensitive to the feelings of others and accepting, in his own view, bunkum from no one. I seem to remember that he was a monk too, though of the travelling type that makes vagabondage a virtue. He was pursuing an extended pilgrimage, meandering along a zigzag route that neglected not a shrine or holy spot, intent, so he said, to reap every possible benefit for "his miserable soul." He paused at this phrase and his face went momentarily expressionless with heartfelt modesty as he lowered his eyes. He and Charlie were sitting around the table after the midday meal. They'd gone begging together that morning, soon after Charlie's friend first arrived. Now there was a discreet burp from the visitor and it was time to hear highlights from some of his adventures on the road.

"Tell me," Charlie piped up scratchily for his oldest pal, "about some of the lands you have visited since we last met." And the stocky man looked up, smiled, and launched forth.

"I think it was during the full-moon festival of the summer solstice, eight . . . no, maybe it was nine years ago that we last met. Yes, I remember we went down by the river and sat near the booths of the iced-drinks salesmen while all about raged the dance and ballyhoo of celebrating humanity. In fact, it's strange that we should be so quiet on this occasion, by contrast—only the two of us together in a room. Hmmm . . . yes, it all comes back so clearly now, the fireworks cascading into the night sky briefly to join the semipermanent stars, the ever-vanishing laughter of children, the flirtatious whirligig of any fête, and the moon . . . the moon placidly smiling down on all of us, young and old alike. . . ."

Charlie's friend rambled on in this discursive manner, building to his theme, and delighting in the exercise of his peculiarly adept vocal cords. At the same time, however, Charlie himself kept knocking, at regular intervals, a spoon against his drinking glass, making a loud ringing noise, so that his friend's narrative sounded, in fact, like this:

"Well, as you may remember, I headed north the next morning, taking the long road towards Banaria, in order that . . ."

Trink!

. "I might stop at the tomb of the great saint Heavababi, which as you no doubt realize is located near the village of . . ."

Trink!

"Peramat, a lovely little spot, which if you've never been to it, I certainly can recommend very highly. It's located in a lush green valley not far from a waterfall where you can . . ."

Trink! Trink!

"Now look here!" Charlie's friend suddenly burst out. "What the devil are you doing with that spoon? You ask me to tell a story and then keep interrupting. What's the matter with you?"

Charlie's eyes grew wide from shock and he sniffed deeply as he reared back in his seat.

"I'm very, very sorry," he said piteously. "I intended no disrespect. You see, it's the wretched rats that steal my food. I was trying to keep them away."

"Keep the rats away?" his friend enquired incredulously.

"Yes," said Charlie, almost on the point of tears. "You see, there's a vicious gang of them that live here, constantly stealing my food—sometimes right before my eyes! Nothing I do ever seems to stop them, and one is so impudent he creeps up and nips my toes at night while I'm asleep in bed. Oh, it's awful, I tell you, and I hate them!"

"Now, now," said Charlie's friend. "I understand the problem. But tell me. Is it one rat who causes most of the trouble, or do they thieve as a team?"

"It's this one particular rat," said Charlie, "who's the worst of the lot. I think he's half-demon, for he can jump so high he flies. There's nowhere in the room I can leave leftovers in my begging bowl that he won't reach. He gets everything."

"Aha!" exclaimed Charlie's friend. "Not for nought does Mrs. Sadili give something for nothing."

"I beg your pardon," said Charlie. "What do you mean?"

KALILA
AND DIMNA

*There are
a number
of Hindus
who make it
their sole
profession
to wander from
one place
to another
relating fables
and stories
which are
very often
utterly devoid
even of common
sense.*

Abbé Dubois

"Don't you know the story of Mrs. Sadili and the sesame seeds?" asked his friend.

"No, no, I'm afraid I don't," replied Charlie.

"Well, put all the remaining food in front of me so I can personally guard it from Super Rat," said Charlie's friend. "Pass me that spoon and glass as well, and you just sit back and relax while I tell it to you."

"All right," said Charlie.

Mrs. Sadili and the Sesame Seeds

"There once was a man named Sadili who wished to
entertain some business friends. He said to his wife,
'Doris, I'd like to invite a few people over for dinner one
night. Will you do the cooking, please?'

Doris said, 'What are you talking about? We barely
have enough money to feed the kids and ourselves, let
alone throw a dinner party. You'll need to work harder
and earn a bit more if you want the luxury of playing
host.'

'Listen, darling,' Mr. Sadili began softly, 'this could
be an important dinner. If so-and-so and so-and-so get
on well together, we could benefit financially. I'm sure
you've probably put by a little something for an emergency or as a treat for the children. Well, *now* is the
time to use it or we risk ending up like the wolf in the
story of "The Wolf Who Wished to Hoard." '

'Oh, yeah?' said Mrs. Sadili. 'And how does that go?'
'Like this,' answered Mr. Sadili.

The Wolf
Who Wished to Hoard

'One day in a forest a mighty archer killed a beautiful
doe. He was carrying her home across his shoulders
when he saw a huge boar grubbing under a tree. Letting the deer's carcass slip quietly to the ground, he
nocked an arrow from his quiver, drew back on his
longbow, exhaled, and let fly. His arrowhead pierced
the wild pig's neck clear through, in one side and out
the other—blood spurting everywhere. With a vicious
grunt the boar spun to beady-eye his killer, ignored his
pain, and charged with flashing tusks—a demon on
the hoof, scrambling for revenge.

Hatred hurled the raging beast through thicket,
briar, and scrub. The transfixed archer had no time to
flee and took the razor tusks full in the gut. Oh, it was a
horror to behold such carnage—the hunter hunted by
the hunted, no pity anywhere. A sudden heave of
bloody neck, and *r-r-rrrip!* the human belly spills life's
gore upon the ground. Two-legs crumples and boar
goes mad with butchery, shaking wild his deadly teeth
until he fades as well; now three dead upon the earth: a
doe, a boar, a man.

All is silence until, within the hour, a famished wolf happens by. He can scarce believe his eyes and counts the bodies more than once. He thinks, "Look at all this food! How did it get here? Oh, lucky, lucky wolf—as you live and breathe! This is certainly your day—of that you may be sure!"

He sprints from corpse to corpse, sniffing the amazing freshness of what he sees, frisky with delight at the nourishment to come. He tumbles across the ground in solitary joy, and then, just as suddenly, while stretching low and forward with an ecstatic smile, he pauses to consider.

"Now, now," he thinks again, and squints his eyes, "just a little calm, if you please, just a little calm. What I should do is ration this bonanza, consume only little bits at a time, conserve the hoard, put by and save for rainy days. Yes, yes—that's it. I'll cache my chewy bunch of human, pig, and deer and make surprise supplies last and last and last. Heh heh heh heh heh!"

The wolf sat up to study the situation and noticed the archer's bow flung to one side.

"Ah, yes," he said to himself. "Little matter of an empty stomach to tend to first, isn't there? Well, I won't be tempted by any of the goodies. No, no! Discipline, that's what's called for—discipline. I'll just have a snack before I begin hiding the bodies."

And so it was that the wolf, unwilling to waste any part of his treasure, tried to have his meat and, if possible, eat it too. He therefore resolved to ease his hunger on what was least delicate, and accordingly positioned his paws around the archer's bow and commenced at

The faces
passing
seemed to him
pale, with
hunger
not physical,
mixture of
brute and
human,
devouring and
defiling:
long claws and
bird mouths,
fat hips and
loins.

Orton and
Halliwell

one tip to nibble upon the gut
string. Minutes later, when
this bowstring suddenly
parted, the bow itself
whipped out with such
rigid force
that it tore
his throat
open and
killed him.'

'Okay, you've made your point,' said Mrs. Sadili after her husband finished his story, 'though I don't see why you had to do it so violently. I have some rice and sesame seeds tucked away, enough probably to feed eight or nine people. I can make these ingredients into a simple but adequate meal. It won't impress anybody, but it will represent hospitality.'

'That's wonderful,' said Mr. Sadili. 'Don't worry. Things will work out, you'll see. Remember these true words of the poet:

What you have enjoy today, don't despair,
When tomorrow comes you'll have your share.'

A few days later, after her husband had invited the appropriate guests, Mrs. Sadili rose early in the morning and began to prepare the party meal. First she took the hairy, black sesame pods and husked them to obtain the small white seeds inside. These she collected in a bowl until all the pods were done. Next she covered the bowl with a piece of muslin, tipped the contents onto a board and spread the seeds out thinly on the fully opened cloth. She took the plank out carefully into her garden and set it down in the sunlight to parch the seeds.

She told her eldest child, a girl of only six, to guard the sesame from any passing birds and returned into the kitchen to tend to other chores. But the child grew dozy in the heat, her attention drifted dreamily across the tops of flowers, her eyelashes fluttered, and soon she nodded lightly off to sleep. The little girl awoke suddenly to the awful sound and sight of a huge yellow dog gulping and wolfing down great slobbering mouthfuls of the precious sesame.

'Mama! Mama!' she shrieked, and burst into a flood of terrified tears. Mrs. Sadili rushed to the rescue, shooed the dog with a shout and a kick that sent it yelping, then soothed her daughter with a hug and many kisses. Even as this crisis was subsiding, Mrs. Sadili knew that on no account could she bring herself to serve the dog-defiled sesame to her guests that evening.

'There, there,' she cooed to her daughter while her mind rapidly picked through the alternative strategies which faced her. 'There, there—it's all over now, dearest. It's all over.'

With her daughter sufficiently recovered, Mrs. Sadili became nothing if not practical. She bundled up all the remaining sesame into the muslin, spun the ends together, slung the parcel over her shoulder and, with her whimpering daughter in tow, headed for the town market. She went straight to the dry-goods stall and started bargaining with the man behind the counter.

'I'd like to make a trade,' she said, unslinging the bundle from her shoulder. 'White sesame for black, measure for measure.' She opened the bundle for his inspection. 'There's nothing wrong with it, as you can see.'

'Why make such a bad trade?' asked the merchant. 'Why don't you keep it for yourself?'

'Let's just say it's not worth anything to me,' answered Mrs. Sadili.

'Okay,' said the merchant as he threw up his hands. 'Suit yourself. Put it on the scales, and I'll give you equal weight in sesame pods.'

And this is exactly what happened. But as soon as Mrs. Sadili had turned to leave with her new bundle, the merchant's neighbour on the next stall leaned over and whispered in his friend's ear, 'There's more here than meets the eye, brother. Not for nought does Mrs. Sadili give something for nothing.' "

*Man
is an animal
that makes
bargains; no
other animal
does this—
one dog does
not change
a bone with
another.*

Adam Smith

"So you see," said Charlie's friend at the end of his story, "there's a reason why Super Rat always reaches your begging bowl." He waggled the spoon in his hand in rhythm to his words. "Your pesky rodent's impudent boldness," he rapped out, "stems from a specific cause. Something gives him his power, and if you'll bring me an axe, I think we can uncover the source of his strength."

"An axe?" enquired Charlie, quizzically screwing up his face. "What for?"

"You'll see," said his friend, as he stood up and pulled his stool back from the table. "We're going to do a little exploratory surgery on your cell, find out what lies hidden behind these walls up the rat holes."

"Right!" exclaimed Charlie, and he too stood and immediately went to fetch the axe from the monastery's woodshed.

An inkling of impending disaster shivered my fur. I watched Charlie's friend stomping around the room, loudly whopping that spoon into his palm as he surveyed all my possible entrances into Charlie's domain. Luckily I wasn't in my main retreat, or things could have gone even worse.

Charlie ran in with the axe. For a moment they conferred with their backs to me. Then there was the most god-almighty sound of smashing skirting board, screeching nails, and blasted plaster you ever heard. The bastards were breaking into my home! My whiskers began to droop when I realized what they would find there. Hidden up that hole where I generally lived was a treasure, a stash of a hundred and thirteen golden dinars which had lain there from long before when I first arrived at the monastery. I had removed the coins from their rotting purse and spread them about on the floor of my abode, for I loved the smooth feel of gold under my feet. I used to revel in the sumptuousness of my rat's nest, skidding back and forth across my treasure or leaping from stack to stack around the sides with demented joy. Sometimes I even tumbled the lot down upon myself in a wanton heap of gold, gold, and more gold until the frenzy of my pleasure reached such a pitch that I foamed at the mouth and passed out from sheer delight. It felt so damned good. I cannot explain why; it wasn't even mine, really. But never mind: it worked, and I always brimmed with confidence because of its constant, nearby presence.

Anyway, here was Charlie's friend going hammer and tongs at the brickwork, using the blunt end of the axe to smash his way in. Suddenly he was right there; six or seven dinars whizzed into the air to ricochet off wall or ceiling. He carefully put the axe aside, and as I watched from across the room, both monks went silently to their knees and began to scrabble through the rubble.

"Gold!" began Charlie's friend in a loud whisper.

"Gold!" echoed Charlie.

"Heh heh," laughed his friend. "Heh heh heh."

"Hee hee," Charlie joined in. "Hee hee hee."

The surge of their laughter mounted with each coin that they robbed from my hideout until I felt swept up in the tide of their mockery and all self-confidence drained out of my heart. News of my plundered home quickly spread to every rat in the community, and a few of my so-called friends crept up a subsidiary tunnel to offer me their condolences.

"Oh, well," said the first fellow to emerge into that side hole from which I was still gloomily watching Charlie and his fat friend pick their way through my gold hoard. "Easy come, easy go, old buddy." I nipped both his ears in a flash, sent him squealing back out the way he'd come in, causing a chattering traffic jam in the tunnel as his hasty exit forced the other gossips to back up and mind their own business. After that they left me alone until their bellies began to growl. Meanwhile, Charlie and friend had snatched away every last one of my coins and sat back down at the table to divide the spoils.

"Here's the magic behind Super Rat's flying leaps," Charlie's friend commented as he flicked the coins back and forth into two even piles. "From now on, he'll be helpless."

He paused for a moment, chuckling to himself as he continued sharing out the booty. Suddenly he laughed and stopped altogether, leapt up with a smug smile brightening his pudgy face, and sang out to Charlie across the table:

> "Super Rat is gone and poor,
> His riches we heap up—
> No longer can he leap about
> For Super Rat's unstuck!"

Charlie giggles in a snaggled-toothed way, looking just like the simpering clod he always was. Meanwhile

Fatso slaps his thigh and shouts out his goofy song again, knocking his seat over as he dashes around the table to get Charlie to join him. He yanks him to his feet and soon both monks are dancing around clasped in a ridiculous embrace like two young schoolboys on a spree and chanting over and over again additional verses such as:

> *"Nyaana nana nan na!*
> *Super Rat's a fink*
> *On the blink on the blink*
> *Nowhere left to slink."*

Needless to say, by this time rats and mice of all shapes and sizes, not to mention various friendly cockroaches, silverfish, and earwigs, are pouring into the room from every conceivable squeeze-hole in order to catch a glimpse of these extraordinary cavortings.

And what could I do? Nothing, it seemed, until this human hysteria had passed. I suppose from their own point of view the peak came when Charlie finally caught the spirit of the thing, and entered into their mood of mischief enough to risk displaying his own meagre talents. From my point of view it was the absolute nadir; nothing could have been worse. It is probably for this reason that I remember the scene most clearly. I can see now that it was one of those moments when truth's mirror pivots to flash you full in the face. What was most shocking was that God chose the likes of Charlie to shine me back myself. I suppose I ought to be grateful, but at the time I hated it. Anyway, Charlie suddenly dropped to one knee, flung his arms

out wide and started to croon in the best mock baritone
his squeaky voice could muster. It sounded terrible but
it sure hit home.

> *"I'm just an ordinary rat*
> *a rodent in the race*
> *trying to find a way*
> *to feed my funny face*
>
> *I'm just an ordinary rat*
> *and very glad of that*
> *no more jumping up and down*
> *leaping all around the town*
>
> *I'm just an ordinary rat*
> *and very glad of thaaat!"*

Can you believe it—Charlie slipping into an act like
that? Fatso goes wild and yowls with delight, thumps
Charlie vigorously on the back until he begins to cough
and splutter.

Well, this stupid taunting put me in none too good a
mood. If they'd carried on much longer I probably
would have attacked blindly, rushed them, and tried to
jump up and bite their faces to pieces and been killed
into the bargain. As it was, I didn't do myself too much
credit with the performance that followed. I was so
angry that all I needed was the barest provocation to
make an utter fool of myself. And let me tell you,
friends: that's exactly what I did.

Things had quieted down. The two monks were sitting at the table again, panting heavily from their gay
exertions.

"Tell you what," gasped the despicable fat one, un-doer of my comfortable life, "we could test it," he continued, "right here." He nodded his head towards that army of curious spectators who remained transfixed along the walls at the other end of the room. "In front of an audience of his own kind," he concluded.

Too puffed to talk further, he simply reached over for Charlie's begging bowl and stood up slowly to hang it on a low nail a few paces away. Then he sat back down again, still breathing heavily. After a few minutes, when he had regained some calm, he called out in a low soft voice:

"Oh, Sooper Raat—come and get it. Oh, Sooper Raaat . . ."

I needed no urging. Damned if this monkoid would make a fool of me. I tore out of there, paws flying against the floor in a scrambling blur. This wasn't even a test, it seemed so easy. The begging bowl was three, maybe three-and-a-half feet up the wall—a cinch. I hunkered down about a foot out at a sharp angle, cocked my back legs, ready to go. Crack! I smashed straight into the wall, tumbled backwards, dizzy. I couldn't believe it: I'd been short! I figured overconfidence had undermined me, shook my head, and set myself up again, much more methodically this time, making sure my balance was right, swaying loosely back and forth on my toes to get the perfect feel. I noticed the silence around me. Suddenly my body triggered into the leap. Hope hoisted me, but not enough. Again I smacked into the wall, scratching frantically with my claws, trying to run the last six or

seven inches against gravity. The floor claimed me, and this time as I lay there dazed, with great thumpings of desperation raging through my heart and head, I heard a chuckling murmur from the spectators. I got up a bit shakily and saw that some were leaving, insect and rodent alike trooping back the way they'd entered. There was a twitter from Charlie's direction. I spun round to catch him and Fatso smirking with delight.

"Hey, Zirac," one of the rats that remained called out, "we're hungry. How about some food?"

This sentiment appealed to the restless crowd, and soon a squealing and chirruping chant swept along the floorboards:

> "Zirac! Jump in the bowl
> Zirac! Feed us some food
> Hurry now
> Move now
> Jump, Zirac, Zirac, jump!"

I was an idiot not to see they did it just for sport. The fallen hero credits not the public's sudden disdain, its appetite for broken idols. What is more tempting than to tear down the mistakenly elevated? And yet, in our frailties, what upliftment of the person, his or her predominance over others, is not but a most temporary affair when death lacerates all distinctions found in life?

This is easy to say in retrospect. At the time I had a strong sense of impending doom, but no understanding of its basis. To recognize that I was simply acting out part of a social mechanism would have upset my concept of free will. And yet here I was, a cog in the whim of others, this time setting up for a last running fling towards that cursed begging bowl.

I knew it was wrong before I even started. My timing felt off, my body awkward, but I couldn't stop. I ran in clumsily, the crowd cheering me on, and I leapt . . . nowhere. It was the worst yet. I stumbled over my own feet, barely leaving the ground and rolling into a help-less ball at the base of the wall. Great ratcalls of deri-sion fell upon me. I didn't wait a second longer, but fled as fast as I could back to my hole. The shiverings began in relative privacy, then the sobs came and soon I was a total wreck undergoing, I suppose, a kind of break-down. No one came to help me.

I huddled in my misery, conserving energy as best I could, waiting for failure's shock to pass. With the re-turn of calm came the gradual reflection that Charlie's hateful friend was probably right; my former gold had indeed been the invisible fuel of my leaping, the pro-pellant of my vigour. I understood that whosoever loses the radiance of wealth finds darkness. Friends and kinfolk no longer see him, for why should they too enter gloom? My mind traipsed down a long corridor of insight, entering, through newly opened doors, dif-ferent offices of truth. I beheld a pattern never before understood by me.

Apparent friendship, I saw, fluctuates with status. Who cannot favour the rich and powerful with kindly attention? Only those still richer and more powerful than they—or who at least consider themselves to be. Beyond such ranking systems, however, lies the wisdom of him or her, either rich or poor, who can truly joke: "Snobbery is beneath me!"

When fortune is in full flood
everyone drinks at the banks of the merry stream
but when the drought comes
its stony bed lies empty.

When nectar fills your flowerhood
like bees they buzz about—
but where are they
when icy winter comes?

I remembered a story told by my grandfather when I was barely more than a hairless squiggle. He was telling it to my mother, who felt pride in the number of her friends, especially now that she was nesting such a healthy brood as my brothers and sisters and me (we were her first batch, seven little ratlets all told). According to my grandfather, a wise person was asked, "How many friends have you?"

"I don't know," he replied, "for as fortune now favours me, heaping me with riches beyond measure, everyone displays friendship and boasts of intimacy. But if adversity should ever kick sand in the eyes of my prosperity, we should have a means of sorting friend from foe. Adversity and distress are the season for testing friends. Most people love wealth and esteem him who has it, but when it slips away so do they vanish."

When the rose flounces her golden skirt in the garden
the nightingale chants her praise in a thousand songs

but when her bloom is scattered by the wind
no one ever hears the name of the rose.

This little poem was wafting through my mind like a
soft breeze stirring sad memories when a sudden
movement made me start. One of my erstwhile friends,
a male I had thought to know quite well, was scurrying
past my hole. I called to him and asked straight out
why he shunned me. He stopped and turned back
slowly, wincing awkwardly as he approached, for this
was one who formerly always gave out as if one moment of my society comprised the capital stock of perpetual happiness. At least he had the courage not to
mince his words.

"Look, Zirac," he began, "it's nothing personal, you
understand? But I'm afraid you've lost it, and there's
nothing more to say. None of us is stupid enough to
flatter a nobody, for what's the profit in that? When
you could tip out the begging bowl we honoured you.
But now . . . well, we all have to live, you know."

He smiled and quickly wiped his whiskers against
each shoulder. Frankly I wasn't that surprised by his
attitude. My little meditation had readied me for such
I-Me-Mying. Nevertheless, I managed some indignation
in my reply.

"How can you talk like that?" I asked. "Is not the
poor rat a king free from the race? Is not joy extra sweet
for him who fears no loss, even breath itself? The poor
overvalue not the loan of life since they hold it near the
edge of balance, keeping always, in their worst misery,
death a near neighbour and even, to the wise, a dear

friend who will repay their debt. While wealth often starts a chain of addiction for more and more, poverty snaps the links that trap the unfree mind, and gratitude for less and less gives perception more precious than any form in life. In short, the poor are free from megalomania and the rampant rages of consume, consume. Thus it has been truly said by the noblest fakirs and seekers:

"Poverty is my boast
Poverty is essential, and except poverty, all is accidental
Poverty is health, and except poverty, all is disease.'"

"Haw haw haw—what a load of rubbish!" my companion exclaimed loudly, and he shook with exaggerated laughter in a manner which hardly seemed polite. "What relation does the unexpected loss of your gold have to the *voluntary* poverty approved by saints and prophets? True poverty implies that a seeker accepts neither the coin of this world nor that of the next—that is to say, he abandons everything so as to acquire everything. 'None arrives at the total save him who has severed himself from the total.' This poverty the dervish displays, while the other pauper is a beggar. The dervish abandons the world, but the world abandons the beggar.

A bread beggar is like a landed fish,
Looks like a fish, but is fled from the sea—
A pauper hankering after dainties but ignoring God:
Place not trays before dead souls."

With this final criticism my so-called friend turned
and sped off, leaving me gawping after his waving tail.
I shook off the mood of helplessness left by his words.
Whatever his view (and certainly his speech had tremendous impact), I simply could not yet abandon all
hope of reclaiming power. Thus it was that I waited
patiently until after dark. Charlie and Fatso had settled down to sleep on their respective pallets, each
having tucked his share of my gold under his pillow. I
crept out into the dim moonlight determined to rob
Charlie, poor simpering fool. The breathing of both
men seemed heavy enough, and I assumed they were
well on their way to the Land of Nod. But I hadn't
reckoned on the downright sneakiness of that fat devil
of a monk. He is lying in wait for me, faking. I'm maybe
six feet from Charlie, plotting how I'm going to ease out
the coins stashed away in a bundle under his head
when *Thwack!* Fatso's walking staff cracks down on
my rump so hard it about splits my hipbone. I scuttle
out of there lickety-split, get back to my hole in such
agony I nearly faint.

Charlie wakes up and through a haze of pain I hear
excited voices as fat friend explains his derring-do. Yet
this distant babbling lasts only a few minutes, and
within an hour or so all is snores again and I creep out
for another try, my stubborn ambition more desperate
than ever. Quite right: poverty was *not* for me—not yet,
anyway; I wasn't giving up a fortune so cheaply.

I sneak along close to the wall and approach Charlie's pillow from a different angle. It doesn't matter; fat
demon is ready for me: *Whack!* This time my head is

knocked sideways into a sudden flash of light. I convulse on the floor, stunned and bleeding from a wide scalp wound, frothing at the mouth and sensing that death is surely next—a twitching wee rat about to vanish into the dark! *Whack! Whack! Whack!* That stick crashes down on the floor about me as I squirm from side to side, the darkness my only friend.

"*Aieee!*" screams Charlie as the banging about his head wakes him. Fatso growls something like "*Shut up!*" or "*Keep still, you idiot!*" I'm not sure which, for I don't even remember scrambling out of there. But somehow I did, and this time when I reached my sanctuary, I passed out, dead to the world.

Next thing I know, it's late morning. I can't open my eyes because they're stuck fast with dried blood, but I can hear the monks moving about. I huddle there listening to these distant human shufflings, suspended between the misery of total failure and the necessity to remain absolutely still or risk tumbling into another abyss of pain. Surprisingly, my perceptions drift light and easy, sail beyond my little life and gain overview. I lived, then, briefly on two levels at once, *in* but not *of* agony's prevailing habitat. I experienced, if you'll pardon the expression, a type of psychic override where disinterested perspective allowed extra clear-headedness. I felt myself hovering like a motionless ghost on the verge of fresh discovery. My pain-paid knowledge proved a truer organ of sight than my former hankering eyes. And what was it I saw? Ah—that is the question most difficult to hold in precision's gripping knot, yet I will try, for this subject labours me by its complexity and I would dearly love to haul it taut.

I nudged death's very brink; with my eyes closed, I saw myself lying there unmoving. And yet I was, in fact, free for the first time in my so-called life. There was no fear, no care, no sense of missing something I ought not to let go by. I was alone; myself, at last, as I really am—just an ordinary rat, competent at some things, hopeless at others. Super Rat was dead. I had a type of pity for him, as one does for anything that wastes potential. I saw his pride, his arrogant falsity which gave him grandiose desires—his greed, in short, for that was his supreme disease—greed for more and more of what he did not need. Such ignorance was the price of pain, and he had spent and spent and spent. Now the burden of hankering care soared free; I lay defeated yet content, a winner of my own war on want. Life alone was all I needed, and I came back to grip it. "Zirac, my boy," I said to myself, "get off your tail. The gold is gone, but what little time you have is left. Get on with it!"

Drink contentment's nectar,
Fill joy in peaceful minds—
Leave goldrushing to the greedy
Who never know repose.
Happiness is health—no more!

No sooner did this thought occur than one dear lady friend happens on the scene. "Eeeek," she squeaks when she sees my curled-up body. I zip back to the here-and-now to be there when the kisses start. My only rat-friend licks blood from furry face until I groan awake. My new life starts. Days later I can just begin to move, thanks to this sweet angel. I have nothing for her except gratitude and willingness to express it, even clumsily. But I must live apart; she has other duties to the tribe. There is sadness when I leave, but no doubt in my mind. We part tenderly. I go into exile, into the desert north of Mahila where I lead a life of bracing hardships. It is there that I first meet King Sharpeyes, a bachelor then, and we survive certain extraordinary experiences. We come to the deserted ruins and I decide to stay; somehow the ghosts suit my needs. Sharpeyes leaves for further adventures until his return years later as leader of a netted flock. In the meantime, solitude has nourished me to new strength of purpose.

At first, I sometimes moped about my loss of glory. But the very thought of gold, combined with the memory of that final beating from Charlie's friend, triggered such nauseating seizures of trembling and quaking in my limbs that soon I banned self-pity. I passed through a series of disgusts, even held militant debates with myself from several different viewpoints. The mound where I lived was like a stage with many entrances, and I used to pop from one to the other to a third or fourth and more, offering fiery speeches, rejoinders, counters, feints, and dodges—tugging at any particularly vexing subject until I had exhausted it or enough of my multiple selves and went down for a sleep. What did it matter? Who was there to hear me in that solitary wilderness? I ranted; I raved. Gradually my strength and self-confidence returned, although I suppose I was at least half mad—vigorously overcompensating, in a way, for my now-known littleness in life. Nevertheless, I rejoiced in the simplicity of my few requirements. I was alone, but I was alive!

Thus it was that when Sharpeyes returned I was like a prisoner too long confined. I knew not how to deal with society's simple joys; I shivered when those pigeons cheered me. Underneath the gruffness, I realized later, was a still-shy rat without community. It is to Shesheen here that I owe thanks for release from self-obsession. She overcame suspicion, and offered trust, and delivered goodness in her way. When I fell back to brood too long on death, aloneness, decay, and dust, she smiled, cocked her black, black head and squawked, "Hello, my little rat! What's got you down?"

And so she brings me here and I tell my story. The reason I do is this: all my life I took and gave little back. I took strength, gold, Charlie's food, adulation, gifts, prestige, status, power, and acclaim; I was Super Rat. But now I am simply Zirac, brother rat, a friend who gives his small capacity if there be any need. True riches, I discover here with you—and you have been kind to listen for so long—are in those links, one creature with another, called friendship. All else in this world is paltry and of no worth.'

There are some who will prefer not to contemplate their animal selves.

Desmond Morris

Deep silence prevailed when Zirac ended his tale. He snuggled backwards into his hole. The air was cool and a crescent moon hung just beyond the fingers of the trees. For a long moment the three friends listened to gently lapping wavelets from the pond and stared up at a star-powdered sky. Finally Slowpoke crunched gravel as he swung around to speak to Zirac.

'I thank you, Ordinary Rat, for such a super tale,' he rumbled softly. 'I've not enjoyed such floods of wonder since my mother's mother—bless her shell—passed on. She used to spin my little nipper brain in swirls as you have done; and another night when we have time I'll try to dredge up gems of hers from my old memory-bin. But now I pay full thanks to you for lending pictures from your life; by them I plainly see the pathway you trod to reach the brightness of your state. I did so love to hear these visions of your past, and hope you will not mind me saying this, that . . . that . . . ho ho! I'm lost: tangled deep in snaky weeds and unable to move from the trap of words! Well, never mind, Zirac, mate. What I have to say is this: ditto here! Birth is dilemma! We all suffer ups, downs, and vapid indifferences—so what else is new for you, for me, and even dear She-sheen? I'll tell you something, however: so long as life shines upon me, mothlike will I whirl in the beams from your beauty. You've grabbed me, you little Sneakfuzz, and I surrender completely—damn all caution and reserve! Come to my armour-plated bosom, rat; gather turtle friendship forever! Stay with me, both of you, and help live out some years! All we have is nothing, as you say, without a friend. Count a thousand friends as one, but reckon one enemy as a thousand.'

Zirac zipped from his burrow with delighted, high-pitched yips and squeaks, and somehow managed to fling his paws around one side of Slowpoke's wrinkled neck. This embrace made Shesheen go so rapturously weak at the knees that she nearly tumbled from her perch.

'Caw!' she squawked at the affectionate entanglement below, flapping her wings to regain balance on the branch. 'Stop it, you two! I swoon from overjoy! I can't bear it! How rich we are now unalone!'

'Ho ho, Lady Primfeathers!' Slowpoke called up from between excited rat-nuzzles to his bony head. 'Always within the bounds of decorum, I assure you, madam— even in the dark. Ha!' Shesheen steadied herself against the tree trunk as these emotional comminglings subsided. 'Enough, Brother Fleabite,' Slowpoke giggled. 'Enough, I say! Take my soul but leave the shell! Stop! Stop! You're tickling me to death. No more!'

Zirac stopped and stood breathless in front of the turtle. 'Sorry, captain,' he said. 'I got carried away.'

'We all did,' laughed Slowpoke. 'Never mind. These little ecstasies are sent to try us. But now I think sleep should carry us away; I'm tired.'

'Hear, hear!' Shesheen cried out wearily from above.

'Agreed,' said Zirac. 'Good night and thank you for your ears,' and he scuttled back to his hole.

'Good night,' called the other two, and soon all was quiet and peaceful.

Next morning the friends awoke to commotion.

Someone was frantically crashing through the underbrush in their direction. Slowpoke slid quickly down
the bank and slipped underwater. Shesheen flew and
hid in the uppermost branches of a tree. Zirac wished
his one-night hole were deeper. Peeking down through
the leaves, Shesheen saw a desperate gazelle bound
into the clearing and freeze like a statue by the edge of
the pond, her lustrous eyes wide with terror, her tense
limbs quivering. The crow flew up high to reconnoitre
and returned a few minutes later when she found that
no one was pursuing the petrified gazelle.

'Zirac! Slowpoke! All clear!' she screeched from the
tree. 'It's only a thirsty gazelle! Zirac! Slowpoke! All
clear! All clear!'

The gazelle's tail twitched pertly and one ear flicked
back towards Shesheen's voice. Surfacing so carefully
in the middle of the pond that he barely made a ripple,
Slowpoke craned his neck and swung his head slowly
about until he spotted the panting gazelle.

'It's all right, Slowpoke,' Shesheen called again from
the tree. 'Just a thirsty gazelle. She's alone.'

But from his vantage point Slowpoke could see that
the gazelle was more than simply thirsty. She remained as if hypnotized by the side of the pond, transfixed by shock, her round eyes unmoving. Her beautiful sandy coat was begrimed by dark streaks and
her tongue lolled from obvious exhaustion. Slowpoke
swam towards her and spoke soothing words.

'Hello there,' he called gently. 'My name is Slowpoke
and this is Black Pond. Won't you stay and take refreshment? The water is cool and clear, so have a drink

or even a bath. Please, be our guest: make yourself comfortable.' By this time Slowpoke, who had reached the bank, waded ashore and stood bow-legged and dripping before the terrified gazelle, his head cocked sideways in a friendly fashion. 'What's your name?' he asked.

The gazelle started violently. *'What?'* she cried, blinking and swallowing. 'Oh!' she said more calmly, but still in a daze, 'I'm Dapple. Hello.'

'Hello, again,' said Slowpoke cheer-fully. 'You're perfectly safe here, so don't worry. Would you like a drink? It will make you feel much better.'

'Yes, please,' said Dapple softly. 'Thank you very much.' Slowpoke lumbered aside and watched the ga-zelle take five tremulous but incredibly dainty steps forward, bend her head, and delicately sip pond water.

'Go on,' said the turtle. 'Have a bath if you want. No one will disturb you.' Dapple raised her head and looked at Slowpoke with her dark, long-lashed houri eyes and crinkled her muzzle into a sad smile. She stepped farther into the shallows.

Meanwhile, Slowpoke went and found Zirac and Shesheen. The three friends quickly agreed to offer the gazelle hospitality. When she had finished her toilet and groomed herself dry in the sun, Slowpoke invited her over to meet the crow and the rat. After initial pleasantries, Dapple told of her escape from hunters who had, with a pack of dogs, attacked her herd the previous afternoon. It was possible she was the only survivor, for she had seen many killed — including all of her immediate family. Although lucky enough to slip through the ambush, she was chased by a horseman and two dogs. Terror rendered her fleet; she ran and ran and ran until she knew not where she was. And when night came, she went on fleeing, the mewling sounds of her dying relatives and herd-friends squeezing the very fibre from her heart. She was alive, yes; but it was as if she fled from some great dark hole in her being, a wound raw and gaping, with ragged edges, determined to suck her in. She had to drag each thought back from sharp memory or risk the flood-gash of grief. Her luck had held, and she was here — empty, but glad to talk to the living who could listen. Huge tears welled slowly from Dapple's languorous eyes and rolled like dewy jewels down her cheeks, but she did not sniff or move.

'There, there, Dapple, dear,' Shesheen cooed. 'Take it easy. It's all over now.' The crow waddled forward and tried to reach up and comfort the gazelle with an outstretched wing. 'There, there,' she said again. 'Take it easy.' Feather brushed on fur.

'Oh, sing aloud, my throat!' Dapple suddenly wailed, her sadness bursting forth in uncontrollable sobs. She crumpled to the ground and cried her heart out while Shesheen, Zirac, and Slowpoke huddled silently around to nuzzle and stroke her. They let her cry and cry and cry, for there was nothing else they could do. After what seemed an interminable anguish, she settled down, flopped to one side with a piteous sigh, and fell into a deep sleep. It was late afternoon before she woke, feeling better. Her new friends consoled her tenderly and begged her to remain with them at Black Pond. She agreed, and over the weeks and months that followed the four animals achieved an easy harmony. Dapple found plenty of nearby grazing, and gradually her sadness receded. Shesheen usually accompanied her, and soon they grew very close. Zirac extended his burrow and explored all around the pond. And Slowpoke? Well, he seemed to spend most of his time sunning himself on his favourite log. But as is the way with all smooth lives, crisis intervened.

One day Dapple and Shesheen failed to show up at the meeting tree by Zirac's burrow. It had become customary for the four friends to gather there every noon, rain or shine, and swap stories, fables, jokes, and personal observations.

'I wonder what's keeping them,' Slowpoke fretted nervously after he and Zirac had waited almost an hour.

'Maybe I should go scout round the fields,' the rat volunteered.

'Well, speak of the devil!' Slowpoke exclaimed, for he had spotted Shesheen swooping towards them.

'She's in a hell of a hurry,' Zirac remarked as the crow threw out her wings and braked furiously, dropping nimbly to the ground beside them.

'Ahoy, Dame Speedfeather,' Slowpoke greeted her. 'Whither the Princess Dapple?'

'Quick, Zirac,' Shesheen panted. 'Get your tail up. Dapple's caught in a snare.'

'Holy Slug Shit,' said Slowpoke. 'Where?'

'Southeast of the pond, maybe half a mile out,' gasped the crow. 'Sorry, Slowpoke. Got to go. It's an emergency.'

'Aye, aye,' said the turtle. 'Off you go. Smooth flying and sharp teeth.'

By now Zirac and Shesheen had flown many times and perfected takeoff and landing procedures which were relatively painless for the rat's tail. They were soon airborne and flew silently until they reached the gazelle, who was lying calmly on her side with one of her rear legs caught firmly in a leather noose. Zirac scampered around to survey the scene.

'Don't worry,' he said to Dapple. 'I'll have you out of there in no time.'

'I'm not worried,' smiled the gazelle. 'I trust your teeth.'

'We've got to hurry,' prodded Shesheen. 'The hunter who set this trap could return any minute.'

'Okay, okay,' said Zirac. 'Let me just ask Dapple a quick question, all right?'

Shesheen shrugged her wings in exasperation, clacked her beak and waddled off, obviously flustered.

'Hey, Dapple,' Zirac said, ignoring the crow. 'How come you, someone I've always observed as being supremely cautious, fell into this trap? What happened?'

'I've been trapped before, you know,' replied Dapple, still smiling. 'Name me the wary genius that tiptoes free from fate. The last time I was captured I became the pet of a prince.'

'The pet of a prince?' enquired Zirac. 'You don't say! Tell us about it!'

Shesheen bounced back. 'This hardly seems the appropriate moment!' she snapped. 'Dapple's in danger, you fool! Chew the thong!'

'Oh, keep your feathers on!' retorted Zirac. 'I'm aware of the situation and am about to begin. I can listen and chew at the same time, you know!'

'Please, you two.' Dapple laughed. 'Stop fighting and relax. It'll be all right, don't worry. I'll tell the story, Zirac, while you work. Shesheen, just calm down and listen; panic solves nothing.'

'That's right!' said Zirac.

'Shhhh,' said the gazelle, and began her story as soon as she felt Zirac's teeth attacking the leather thong.

The Pet of a Prince

'When I was a fawn barely three months from my mother's womb I already ran precociously well—even for a gazelle. I adored the clean freedom of flashing my limbs in air over ground rough or smooth. But I knew nothing about traps or snares or the wiliness of men. One day I wandered too far from the herd and, while leaping about with the carefree friskiness of youth—ignoring warning cries from the older females, including even my dear mother—I tumbled into a netted pit and became hopelessly entangled.

The hunter who caught me was a retainer to The Royal Household and eventually I was presented to The King, who gave me to his son, a boy of eleven or twelve. The Prince delighted in my company in his rather rough, spoiled way. He petted me and stuffed me full of my favourite foods. He also hung his arms around my neck; pulled my ears, nose, lips, eyelashes, and tail; stuck his fingers in any of my body's orifices whenever he felt like it; and rubbed disgustingly sweet perfumes into my coat. His spifflications grew so unbearable that one night during a storm my feelings suddenly erupted. I was hiding under The Prince's bed watching jagged lightning flash against the dark, swift-running clouds. There was a shattering, God-Almighty doom-crack, then violent crash of thunder, and I cried out, "O Fate, when again will I run with the haphazard herd, gazelles driven by the wind and rain?"

"Who said that?" called out The Prince. I had forgotten he was sleeping on the mattress above. "Who spoke?" he asked again, lighting a candle and searching all about the room until he found me shivering under his bed. "Dapple?" he asked, for it was he who gave me that name. "Dapple?" he repeated, his eyes widening behind the flickering flame.

Something fragile seemed to shift deep inside The Prince. "My gazelle spoke to me," he mumbled, and stood upright. "My gazelle spoke to me!" he exclaimed, louder this time. Then he flung his arms apart, hurling the lit candle and its holder right across the room, and shrieked, *"Dapple spoke to me!"* By the time his servants arrived to grab him he was screaming like an idiot from the open window, ranting and raving into the storm.

They had to bind him with silken sashes to keep him down in bed. He was feverish and hysterical. The King came in the middle of the night and was dreadfully upset. On and on The Prince babbled about his talking gazelle. I was beaten and kicked about the room, for it was assumed I had caused his madness in some unaccountable way. Uproar reigned all night.

Morning brought doctor after doctor, all impotent to diagnose or treat The Prince's malady—despite stupendous rewards promised by The King. Finally an old medicine man appeared, one reputedly able to read signs.

"You stupid people!" he roared as soon as he was admitted into the room. "What do you mean by beating this poor gazelle!" He rushed over and gathered me tenderly into his arms. The King raised his palm to halt servants from immediately ejecting such an unruly person. We approached The Prince's bed.

"You abominable child," the shaman began fiercely, fixing the boy with a terrible glare, "of course your gazelle spoke to you! Don't you realize that all animals can speak? But they never do so in the company of pitiful humans! This poor creature of God spoke her heart's desire, forgetting you were there. The storm stirred yearnings for her own kind, and she truly spoke the words you heard: 'O Fate, when again will I run with the haphazard herd, gazelles driven by the wind and rain?' So there is nothing wrong with you. This illness is all pretence in the mind. I'm going to count to three, untie you, and you will be permanently cured of this psychosomatic nonsense."

The old man put me down and counted to three. He loosened The Prince's bonds and said, "Now get up and get on with it! There's nothing the matter with you!" The boy rose and indeed was cured. A huge smile spread across his young face, and The King leapt forward to clasp him to his bosom.

The old medicine man refused any reward. "I don't want your gold," he said to The King. "I want your understanding." He left the palace and I never saw him again. The next day, after I had been pampered by The Prince as never before, I was taken to the spot of my capture and released. Soon I rejoined my herd and lived happily for many years until the calamity which sped me here!'

'Well, it's all over now,' Zirac said, after the gazelle had finished her story. 'You're free! Stand up and run, Dapple, dear.'

The suggestion was irresistible. She stood and kicked off the rat-chewed noose in one graceful motion and sprang forward a full thirty feet in a single spectacular bound, turned, and bestowed a devastatingly demure, dark-eyed look of smiling thanks upon the rat and crow, then set off in a slow parade of exquisitely moving beauty, prancing and pirouetting gracefully around them in a large circle. 'Oh!' she cried, stopping suddenly and drawing back, startled by something in front of her.

'Ho ho ho!' rumbled a familiar voice from deep in the grass. 'So we're all right, are we, Princess Dapple? Aye, that's good news, it is, aye.' The rat and the crow sped over. Dapple could only smile.

'What are *you* doing here, you mad turtle?' demanded Zirac. 'This isn't a picnic! What happens if Dapple's snare-setter appears while you're trundling about, you daft beast?'

'That's right,' Shesheen joined in. 'You were silly to come.'

'Ho ho,' rumbled Slowpoke good-naturedly. 'And whose life is worth a spit bubble without friends? I choked with anxiety at the thought of danger to Dapple, and could not keep away. Loveless life is stripped of joy like the leafless tree; lazy, we perish. I came to give when there was need, not later when there was none.'

The end of Slowpoke's speech coincided with the ar-

rival of a human hunter. Dapple bounded off. She-sheen flew away. Zirac hid in the grass. Slowpoke ran as best he could.

'What the hell is going on here?' the hunter said out loud, for he had seen the crow and the gazelle. Stooping to inspect his severed snare and thinking it very strange, he heard Slowpoke trying to escape and ran over to investigate.

'Aha!' he said to the struggling turtle. 'Fate robs me of one prey but gives me another. Well, turtle soup is better than nothing.' Pulling from the earth the stake which had secured his snare, he flipped Slowpoke onto his back and tied his stubby legs to the stake with the leather thong. Then he slung the turtle over his shoulder and strode off.

The three remaining friends soon regrouped. Dapple and Shesheen found Zirac writhing on the ground in an excess of agony.

'Oh cruel Fate! Dirty Destiny! God! Random Chance! Invisible Force! Variable Factor!' he groaned. 'Why hammer my life so thin with disaster, one blow after another? I lost money, strength, status, home—and now Slowpoke! Beat the crippled! Starve the hungry! Smite all downtrodden ones! Calamity runs amok; berserker goes the time!'

'And you certainly are wasting it with such eloquent rubbish!' Shesheen interrupted testily. 'Give your face a rest, Scruffy. Now's the time for action, not words. Dapple and I need your help.'

Zirac peered up at his friends sheepishly, then scrambled to his feet. 'You're right,' he said to Shesheen,

looking her straight in the eye. 'Your criticism is an astringent. Here I am, done moaning. What can I do?'

'Dapple and I need your teeth, of course,' said the crow. 'Here's our plan: we will sneak ahead of the hunter to that point on his path nearest the pond. You must run after him now. Dapple will play dead and I will act the carrion crow, seemingly pecking at her eyes. Our hope is that this decoy will attract the hunter's curiosity. He will drop Slowpoke to investigate, and then you'll nip his bonds so he can escape.'

'I like it,' said Zirac. 'Let's go!'

Except for one or two details, the rescue worked exactly to plan. Zirac never chewed faster and Slowpoke positively galloped for safety in the pond. When the hunter approached gazelle and crow, Shesheen flapped leisurely away from the supposed carcass, then suddenly veered in the air and swooped at his face with outstretched talons, cawing viciously. This experience unnerved the poor man considerably and, more important, gained time for swift-lumbering Slowpoke. Then the miserable human could find no dead gazelle, for Dapple had vanished during Shesheen's diversion. He began to peer about apprehensively as if the place might be haunted or enchanted. When he discovered Slowpoke gone, he needed no further convincing. 'Aaaaahhhhhhh!' he began to cry in terror as he ran away, fearful lest some demon jump him.

Thus it was that Black Pond became taboo to men. Terrible rumours about this place spread to many lands. And since no one dared to bother them, the four friends lived happily ever after.

The children liked her own stories best. "Something from your own head, Mother," they would beg, and she would wrinkle up her brow and pretend to think hard, then begin: "Once upon a time."

Flora Thompson

Doctor's Orders

*There
she took out
a hugeous
silver book,
in the shape
of a half-tierce,
or hogshead,
of sentences,
and, having
filled it at
the fountain,
said to him,
The phi-
losophers,
preachers
and doctors
of your world
feed you up
with fine words
and cant
at the ears;
now, here we
really incorp-
orate our pre-
cepts at the
mouth. There-
fore I'll not
say to you,
read this chap-
ter, see this
gloss, no, I
say to you
taste me this
fine chapter,
swallow me
this rare
gloss.*

Rabelais

There was a silence after Bidpai ended the tale of *Zirac and Friends*, and a look of bemused contentment on the face of King Dabschelim. Once again the floor candles glistened in their cylindrical brass holders, their soft flames wavering gently in the calm evening air.

Bidpai reached for a glass of water and took a long sip to refresh himself. Then, while their mood hovered within delicate alignment to possibility, he leaned forward and made the following statement. It was nearly twilight, and the king never forgot the impact of the old man's words.

"Your Majesty," said Bidpai, "I must now inform you that I have told all I can of the stories illustrating King Houschenk's precepts. To be sure, there are many more stories, and, in fact, some tellers claim the storehouse is limitless, being constantly replenished. But in your own case, Sire, the cornucopia must, for a time, cease. There is now an operative prohibition upon my reciting more.

" 'Why is that?' you will naturally want to ask, and

257

so I shall answer you. Kings are seldom denied the objects of their desire. But please remember that here we are dealing with a type of medicine, and not a sweetmeat for your royal delectation. This medicine has its own requirements of operation, Your Majesty, and one of these is time—time to gain effect. We must observe, therefore, whether the stories of the past two days act beneficially on your humanity. Meanwhile, you could do worse than to repeat to yourself, silently or aloud, in your own words, whatever you remember of what you've heard—but without the added process of interpretation. I must emphasize this last point: my stories require, at this stage, no extra commentary, wretched imaginings, or vapid guesswork by you, me, or anyone else. The very worst habit would be that of moralizing away the effective substance. Thus the urge to tag tidy little rationalizations, persuasive formulas, intellectual summaries, symbolical labels, or any other convenient pigeon-holing device, must be steadfastly resisted. Mental encapsulation perverts the medicine, rendering it impotent. It amounts to a bypass around the story's true destination; to explain away is to forget. It is also a type of hypocrisy—poisonous, an antidote to truth. Thus, let the stories which you can remember do their own work by their very diversity. Familiarize yourself with them, but fiddle with them not. Have I made myself quite clear on this point, Your Royal Highness?''

"Yes, yes," said the king, "most overabundantly! And for God's sake, drop the honorifics. Just call me Dabschelim from now on—please!" The king was agitated and stood up quickly, shoving his easy chair backwards so that it scraped loudly across the tiled floor. He walked over towards a fili-gree window and peered down into the garden, noticing one particular pink rosebush for no especial reason.

"What, Your Majesty?" Bidpai in-quired of Dabschelim's back, "and risk being Schanzabeh to your lion, or ex-citing a Dimna within the court? No, thank you, Sire, I cannot gamble with such familiarity. You, Sir, are The King and I the subject; so it is written and thus I conduct myself."

"Oh, I suppose you're right," Dabschelim said, turning around. Now he looked sad and a bit pale. "But what about the remainder of Houschenk's pre-cepts: when will you tell me the rest of the stories?"

Bidpai rose from his seat, bowed, and smiling kindly, moved closer to the king. He bowed again and, clasp-ing his hands loosely behind his back, leaned forward and spoke gently as follows:

"Please excuse the vigour of my speech, Your Maj-esty, but everything will occur within its due course. Fear not, and forestall pernicious imagination. Once I am sure the medication is working, we can proceed. You have now received approximately one-half of what I bring. To give more now risks an overdose, to the singular detriment of the patient and, to be sure, all his subjects also. In the meantime, we must wait and fol-low the power of patience, which is, after all, part of the treatment. When the appropriate signs materialize, I shall, you may be sure, request another audience, and you, if you wish, may hear the final dose of stories. Remember that it is the improvement of kings which is our goal; there are certain things that you, Sire, as a king, must work out alone in this enterprise.

"Thus it is, Your Majesty, that I must now request, for your own benefit, a leave of absence. Allow me and my wife to return to our normal home while you pursue kingly business as best you can. Let us keep a bond of calm silence upon this discussion; do not babble this medicine about in idle dissipation, but husband its secret, Sire—focus its strength in your heart for you and you alone. The time to tell will come. Please do not seek me out. Rather keep steady courage and hold firm that fort of patience. But now you are probably very tired, and so I say, Adieu!"

And with that old-fashioned word of parting, Bidpai, for the time being at least, turned and walked out of King Dabschelim's life.

*A*fterword

This book is heavily indebted to the scholarship of others. The mainstreams of the Bidpai pedigree flow from Sanskrit, Arabic, Syriac, and Persian versions. I do not read or speak any of these languages. Therefore I relied on the following translations into English:

SANSKRIT F. Edgerton, *Panchatantra,* Allen & Unwin, London, 1965.
ARABIC Rev. Wyndham Knatchbull, *Kalila and Dimna,* W. Baxter, Oxford, 1819.
PERSIAN Arthur N. Wollaston, *The Anwar-i-Suhaili, or The Lights of Canopus,* John Murray, London, 1904.
SYRIAC I.G.N. Keith-Falconer, *Kalilah and Dimnah,* Cambridge University Press, Cambridge, 1885.

In addition, I drew from:

A.S.P. Ayyar's *Panchatantra and Hitopadesa Stories,* D. B. Taraporevala Sons & Co., Bombay, 1931.
Anon., *The Fables of Pilpay,* revised edition, Frederick Warne & Co. Ltd., London, 1886.
Francis Johnson's *Hitopadesa,* Chapman and Hall, London, 1928.

Especial mention must be made of the neglected English classic by Sir Thomas North, *The Morall Philosophie of*

Doni, 1570—the very first penetration by Bidpai into our language. I worked from the reprint of 1888 edited by Joseph Jacobs. Jacobs's introduction to North's version (which relates, against a garbled Christo-European setting, the Kalila and Dimna story in pungent Renaissance prose) remains, despite its Victorian bias, an excellent introductory commentary to the Bidpai phenomenon. Vital supplementary information, however, will be found in the introductions by Edgerton and Keith-Falconer.

These eight versions, each useful in some way, comprised my materials. I studied them until a master template began to emerge. I wanted to write the truest story for a modern audience. It is here that my aim as an apprentice storyteller diverges from that of the traditional scholar. That the *Panchatantra* predates the *Anwar-i-Suhaili* is, to my mind, irrelevant. Both are remarkable documents, each for its time, place, and audience. But as far as the modern layperson is concerned, it's no longer a question of chicken and egg, but of chicken bones. The object here, then, has been to reanimate a living chicken which everybody can enjoy in one way or another. Some hints of the historical savouriness of parts of this bird were given by Rumi: "Seek the story from Kalila, and search out the moral in the story."*

* See Volume 1, *The Mathnawi of Jalalud'ddin Rumi,* translated by R. A. Nicholson, Luzac & Co. Ltd., London, 1977, pp. 50-75. Also "Kalilah wa Dimnah" in *The Encyclopaedia of Islam,* Luzac & Co. Ltd., London, 1927, pp. 694-698.

Also *Hindu Manners, Customs and Ceremonies,* Abbé J. A. Dubois, translated by Henry K. Beauchamp, Oxford, Clarendon Press, 1906, pp. 433-474.

And for background, *Godmen of India* by Peter Brent, Allen Lane, London, 1972; as well as *Kautilya's Arthaśāstra,* translated by Dr. R. Shamasastry, Wesleyan Mission Press, Mysore, 1923.

This book would not have been possible without the generous help of others. Special votes of thanks are due to Idries Shah for giving me the idea; to Oliver Hoare for his encouragement over many years; to John Wynne Williams for his faith despite the odds; to Mrs. Jill Swart, Secretary to the Library Committee of the Royal Anthropological Institute, for allowing me access to the unpublished (and incomplete) manuscript of Mir Bahadur's *Alhlak-i-Hindi* ("The Tales of Pilpay") from the *Hitopadesa,* translated from the Hindustani by Sir Richard Burton in 1847; to Yasin Safadi, Head of the Arabic Section in the Department of Oriental Manuscripts and Printed Books at the British Library, for his help to Margaret Kilrenny in allowing access to rare illustrated manuscripts of Bidpai's Fables; and to Dr. Esin Atil, Curator of Islamic Art at the Freer Gallery, for kindly referring us to the marvellous illustrations in the MS Pocock 400 at the Bodleian Library, Oxford.

"Mine are the weaknesses; the strengths belong to others."

R.W.

Cellardyke, 1979.

A NOTE ON THE TYPE

The text of this book was filmset in a typeface called Bookman. The original cutting of Bookman was made in the 1850's by Messrs. Miller & Richard of Edinburgh. Essentially the face was a weighted version of the popular Miller & Richard old-style roman and it was probably at first intended to serve for display headings only. Because of its exceptional legibility, however, it quickly won wide acceptance for use as a text type.

Composed by New England Typographic Service Inc.,
Bloomfield, Connecticut.
Printed and bound by The Murray Printing Company,
Forge Village, Massachusetts.
Designed by Betty Anderson